Stop the Clock!

A book about Time
What is it? Is it real? Did it start at some point?
Has it ever stopped?

By

Lovemore T Kuwana

Foreword by Dr T Makoni

Stop the Clock!

First Edition 2015

Cover Design & Author Photograph : Adrenalin Advertising Harare
Published by : Babysteps Publishing Limited
Edited by : Simba Kunedzimwe
Copyedited by : Wycliff Chiunda

Contact of the Author : ltkuwana@gmail.com

ISBN-13: 978-1518605826

ISBN-10: 1518605826

Copyright Material used in this book:

Dedication

This work is dedicated to two special people in my life, Eva and Willard Kuwana - my parents. I am thankful to God that he has allowed me to complete this work and kept you alive to witness it. I count it a privilege and a blessing to have you in my life. May He give you more years with us and witness God's grace through this work.

To

Margaret Sigola, Medes, Constance and Judith Pangeti, my mothers, this is for you also. I thank God for all of you, and having kept you all to witness this. I am thoroughly blessed to be your son. May God give you more happiness from this day forth!

To everything,

there is a season,

and a TIME

to every purpose under the heaven:

Table of Contents

Copyright Page ii

Dedication Page iii

Epigraphy page iv

Table of Contents v

Endorsements for the book vii

Foreword ix

Preface xiv

Acknowledgements xviii

Introduction **1**

Chapter 1 – Time and Leadership **3**

Chapter 2 -Transitional Phases of Time for a Purposeful life **11**

Chapter 3 - The cost of lost time **19**

Chapter 4 - Develop a time-conscious Mind **26**

Chapter 5 - Develop a lifelong 'budget' for your time **39**

Chapter 6 - Even Business should develop a time-conscious culture **56**

Chapter 7 - Its foundation in God **69**

Chapter 8 – Could time have existed before the beginning? **73**

Chapter 9 - But is the beginning real? **76**

Chapter 10 - Your life-long plan should not be done in isolation **81**

Chapter 11 - But if we say God created time, when did he do that? **93**

Chapter 12 - Time was first 'creation' to be conferred with dominion **100**

Chapter 13 - Time is the most obedient creation of God **105**

Chapter 14 - What was God's purpose in inventing time? **112**

Chapter 15 - Time has a Spiritual Mandate to fulfill **116**

Chapter 16 - Time has Physical Mandate to fulfill **127**

Chapter 17 - What the 'great' minds had to say about Time **135**

Chapter 18 - Are we destined to fail against time? **143**

Chapter 19 - Time and Chance **150**

Chapter 20 - Time and Faith **155**

Chapter 21 - Existing past your physical time **161**

Chapter 22 - Can you live longer than your time? **164**

Chapter 23 – Conclusion **171**

Endorsements for the book

"The subject of time and how we manage it is both fascinating and vital if we are to achieve the God-given mandate that we all carry as individuals and as families. Our attitude towards this resource determines whether we achieve anything of substance in our lifetime that we could pass on to generations after us. This book is a reminder and a useful guide on the importance of effective time management. We should live our lives knowing that our time here on earth is finite. The gap between birth and death has expectations in terms of end results. As you read this book, let it not be for merely increasing your formal knowledge about time but make this book a tool that triggers the transformation of your time management."

Rabison Shumba (Author, Speaker, Coach)
www.rabisonshumba.com
Harare, Zimbabwe

The issue of time is critical from the moment one is born, to the moment they die. The Psalmist wrote, "So *teach us to number our days, that we may apply our hearts to wisdom.*" The proper handling of time is the beginning of wisdom application. In this book, the author goes into depth discussing the subject of time from many angles. This book will give you a deep understanding of 'time', and equip you with practical methods that you can apply to be better aligned with time, and yield greater results in this life. Time is linked to purpose, and as you understand and apply these things, you will fulfill your purpose in life.

Lovemore. T. Kuwana has invested 'Time' in researching and writing on this subject. It is hard to find another book with all this information put in one place. As you read it, you will surely be enlightened.

Advocate Charles Magaiza
(Author, Apostle and Marketplace Leader)
www.puroseclinic.com

I must confess that this is profound. The work by Lovemore T Kuwana on this contentious subject of 'Time' is the clearest, most biblically framed, and the most compelling text that I have ever encountered. It has had an influence on the way I have now become conscious of time in my everyday life. He makes it clear that time can never be recycled, and so, once gone; it's gone for good. Take stock today of how you have used yours! Consider having this book as a manual or guide to the way you handle your own time. I would recommend this book without hesitation for its remarkably clear, strong basis and practical message to any person wishing for a blissful life.

Reverend Tigere Nyamakawo

Foreword

Time crunch; Time constraints; Shortage of time. These are all too familiar terms. When we are born, we assume that we are equipped with 'time' enough to accomplish everything we wish for. But alas! As we journey along, we begin to realise that so little of it is already left, and yet still so much purpose to fulfill. What has happened to all that time? Could it then be that in actual fact, God did not or does not assign enough of it to each of us? Or are we the cause of this crisis? Why do people regret the usage of their time at their deathbeds? There must be a way out of this web surely.

Every one of us is birthed into time without choice whether to face it or not. Once born, it is do or die. Would you rather then, face it unprepared, or is it the application of wisdom to find a way to contend with it? This book recognises that time had a beginning, and attributes that beginning to God. It seeks to prove that God is the ultimate source of time and hence the only power with absolute authority and control over it. One cannot successfully work within 'time' without being overwhelmed by it unless he recognises this fact, admit to learning from God, master and practice the principles that govern time.

This book provides that foundation and seeks to inspire the effort to master it, by studying in depth; the perceptions, origins, history, the secrets, characteristics etc. of time, in order to be equipped to develop a strategy to optimally use it for the benefit of mankind and for God's glory. From the above background, we can begin to acknowledge and appreciate the inevitable need of this strategy to confront time, in every single person's life. This book prescribes at least some kind of systematic way of planning for your time and offers the guidelines and recommendations to follow, in crafting this strategy.

There can never be a 'one-size-fits-all' kinds of prescription to this endeavour, as we all have unique paths to follow in life, and our days are not numbered the same. No two people are exactly the same. We realise that purpose is the factor that separates any two people, and this occasions each man to pursue his own path and adopt a strategy aligned to the purpose of their existence. So the book takes its time, to justify 'purpose' and how, knowing yours, will lead to better use of time, and avoiding the all too often regret on the death bed. A fulfilled and satisfying end is only guaranteed when 'purpose' has been accomplished. There is a season (time) for everything under the sun. Life places demands on every drop of our every hour, minute, second, etc. As such we cannot afford any waste, for if this happens, then it means one or more aspects of our purpose will have been deprived of its allocation. If you hadn't realised this, start reflecting on it right now. The various aspects of our lives should be accorded their meaningful share. Learning and pursuing the art of optimising one's time is therefore, crucial and should be a lifetime commitment. So once one is convinced of one's purpose in life, they should be able to align their 'time strategy' to their purpose, thereby optimising its usage.

One should be able to tell, what milestones in life, they should have covered by the time they are 'such' an age. This ensures that you have a personal drive from within yourself, to motivate you each day to wake up and face time and what it brings to you. With this kind of planning, very little time drifts into the domains of wasted time. Many people miss the fact that time is the currency of life which as an asset should be jealously guarded and carefully managed. As such any time wasted, registers as a lost opportunity. As some wise sage once said, "Opportunities of a lifetime should be seized within the lifetime of that opportunity." You let time slip, so too does your opportunity to flourish.

The biggest pitfall and which leads to mediocrity among people is a lack of respect for time. Time ought to be respected and highly esteemed. Any attitude, to the contrary, is detrimental to your progress and success. Developing a time-conscious mind should be the foremost passion of any man wishing to take charge of their own life. Lovemore, through this book, offers unique and practical strategies of engaging your mind in striving to achieve this goal. He brings forth the idea that Time Consciousness should be an attribute driven from the subconscious mind. Where you do not have to think about it; you just act 'time consciously' as programmed in your mind without your conscious effort. He takes time to discuss simple but practical techniques that will help re- orienting our minds towards a time-conscious mind because naturally, our 'being' gravitates towards comfort, and comfort has little regard for time, which leads us away from being time conscious.

Without a doubt, time management is critical for both self-leadership and general leadership. To be an effective leader in society, one has to begin with mastering oneself and committing to the discipline that respects values of good time management. I have observed leaders, whether as pastors or business people who are so casual when it comes to 'time'; a first sign of bad leadership. They are never on time, and show very little respect for it. Imagine the result, if such a person were to lead a time cultured people. He would certainly frustrate the bunch out of his church or business or whatever association. Should they decide to stay on, they will make up their mind not to submit to you in that area! The quality of a person's leadership is to a greater extent, affected by the way, he manages his time. Lack of respect for 'good time values' compromises leadership. Integrity is at stake. As Lovemore puts it "time confers authority on the one who demonstrates the most regard for it in any given situation" all the time. I implore on leaders never to allow this situation to happen to them, and to strive always to lead from the front.

Turning to business, well managed time results in increased business profitability, this goes without saying. Any asset possessed by a business, acquired in the course of business, is to a greater extent the result of well managed time, as Lovemore puts it. It should be in the interest of management and the business at large therefore, to ensure implementation of efficient systems that reflect good time values and its management. The author offers, an array of unique tactics that can be exploited by business managers to align time usage to the objectives of the company and achieve good results, with savings significant enough to warrant the effort.

One day, time shall come to an end, just as it came into being, and even science stands ready to confirm this, and so does logic. So before this happens, time has to fulfill two obligations;
1. Its physical mandate, that of causing our physical existence to subsist, and 2. The spiritual mandate, which gives an opportunity for us to decide the quality of life we wish to assume when time eventually ends. In both these scenarios, the book proves that our best chance of facing time is when we are covered by God. In His wisdom, he has put systems to guard and prosper us, as we come face to face with time. He stands ready to defend us against its whims. The message is God knows time better than anyone of us. He has shown a soft spot for mankind over all creation from before the beginning, and so with him, we can defy time. Talk about faith, talk about chance, talk about legacy, God has it all lined up for those prepared to take advantage of these tools and learn from his own strategy.

As a businessperson, a pastor, and family man, I fully appreciated the immense importance of the subject matter. We are stewards of this asset, meaning that, at some point we shall be called to account. Time is a gift that we are granted by God, while our constructive use of it in accomplishing our life assignments is our tribute to Him. The unwritten challenge within this book is simply this: "Honour God and bless humanity with your time."

Well done Lovemore for this contribution to the world on such a vital topic. I highly recommend this book to readers who are serious about their life-calling, their business and their spiritual impact. While it's written from a biblical world view this book will surely benefit any person who dares to read it.

Dr T. A. Makoni
(Author, Business Lecturer, Consultant, Dental Practitioner, and Pastor)
June 2015, Harare

Preface
"What about time"?

This was the most common question that I got every time I shared my dream about my intention to write a book about 'Time'. In fact, it was the first question coming out of every single mouth, of those I shared the subject with. You are probably asking the same question right now. The inquisitive look on people's faces, as they asked, confirmed to me that it must have been somewhat a strange subject or should I say unfamiliar topic, to write about. It looked like people had an idea, of the depth and scope of this subject. This I could tell by the follow-up questions, which proved quite learned, on the subject I must say.

How much depth though, I could not really establish. This prompted me to think hard and decide on the best way I could address that popular question. To be frank, I had no idea either. I wished I had a more satisfying answer. I did not know at the time, the direction the book was going to take. So as I proceeded with that objective, it became clearer to me that, the task at hand was not as easy as I had thought. I needed to dive deep, and come out with plausible and satisfying answers from there. After the whole experience, let me be the first also to admit that indeed time is most evasive, complex, amazing, etc., perhaps we may never even really come to the fullest knowledge and understanding of it, but have this assurance, as you read, that I did my best in trying to uncover some of the hidden mysteries about time.

The book you are reading today is a product of wide consultation and research into the subject. I would have loved to share with you, the pains and struggles and even the joys of piecing this work together, but that may derail our focus for now, and so, let's agree to leave it for another day. However, allow me to share briefly, my biggest challenge as I sat to write.

Let me from the onset make this confession, that 'time', has baffled even the greatest 'minds' that have traversed the face of the earth, and seemed to have eluded even them. As far as I am aware, I believe, none of even these 'giant minds' succeeded in becoming "masters" of 'time' during their lifetime. That thought, was my challenge! How could I successfully try in such a field? Even to this day, modern scientists have no common position on the accuracy of some long-established works on the subject, even by world renowned geniuses such as Plato, Aristotle, Albert Einstein, and so on.

None of them could really claim to have gotten to the bottom of it and emerged the victor. Towards the end of the book, as we wind down, we shall look at some of the admissions made by these geniuses in their efforts to crack this phenomenon. This dilemma alone should be humanity's primary motivation and greatest resolve in confronting time with stubborn determination. For what manner of 'substance' is this, that it can elude the minds and meditation of mankind forever? I dare challenge it, and humanity to arise and face it. Will it be conquered one of these days?

As you read this book, do not read it to race to the end. What I am trying to achieve in this work is a life time's contribution to humanity. I wish for anybody, who by the grace of God finds this book in their hands, to find enlightenment, to be transformed completely to live a positive life whose effect on others will be felt even years after their departure from our beloved earth. It is not my intention to be judgmental or appear to attack any person or certain societal groups. All my contributions are meant for the good and seek to help those who choose to be influenced by this work. It is also worth mentioning that as I started writing this book, I told myself I would be humbled by, and regard highly anybody who would land this book into their hands, and be able to read it, regardless of race, nationality, geographical location or religion.

And so as I started writing, I purposed in my mind that this book needed to be as neutral as it could possibly be. I wanted to tackle this issue without a single mention or bias of my religious beliefs. And to my surprise, I couldn't go far, after just a few pages, I got stuck. How could I have ever attempted to explain 'time' without talking about God? No amount of shrewdness could have allowed me to proceed. Any other alternative explanation that I could think of would come to a dead end without having covered much ground.

I will confess and challenge anybody that it is impossible to talk about time and not talk about God or a divine being. The moment, I accepted this fact; things just fell in place. I was amazed. It is true, that facts are stubborn; the truth cannot be altered. Time finds its origins in God, and He placed it in the universe for his purposes. That is the fact.

So what you then find in this book is truly and genuinely what I believe to be true. This book speaks to me as much as I hope it will speak to you. Unfortunately, (for that wish to be neutral), I found no other credible explanation of time, and so, the whole book is premised on God, as The Creator and one who has absolute authority over time.

By choosing to read this book, whatever has led you to it, has led you to a path leading to a life of fulfillment both in this life and the life after death. This is a journey you have started. Once you read this book, you can never maintain the same attitude towards time again, even if you won't accept all or some of the teachings in it.

It's a process to master the game of time, and once you have perfected the art, use it to your advantage. It's a lifelong commitment. So as you read, do not expect to have mastered these things by the moment you finish reading the book. Keep it as a manual and make reference to it as you journey along.

Recommend it to friends and relatives. Read it once, read it twice, read it again and again. Time consciousness takes time to build. Be patient with yourself and encourage your own self. You will make it.

Lovemore T Kuwana

Acknowledgements

To God, the Master of Purpose. The Creator of all things. The Only "Being" that rules time. To you be all glory and honour. As I traversed the landscape of this journey, I marveled at your works. A real Genius, I am left in awe at the discoveries of your greatness. Nothing can fully describe you God. You placed everything where it is for a purpose, and I am blessed to have been placed to write this book. Thank you for enabling me and helping me to finish this work.

To be quite frank, many people deserve to be acknowledged in coming up with this book. Some may not even know that my interaction with them gave me insights into the subject. In your various ways, and capacities you made this possible guys. I want this blanket expression of my gratitude to cover every individual who contributed to this work in any way. I am indebted to you and pray that God the Almighty will enable me to reciprocate the favour one day. May God richly bless you all!

Allow me the privilege to distinguish a few individuals for their outstanding contribution to my book.

Dr Tafadzwa Makoni, thank you for believing in me and accepting to do my foreword, even though you knew very little about me. Apart from this, I will forever cherish the guidance you gave throughout the project. God bless you.

Rabison Shumba – Thanks for endorsing my book. Your works are an inspiration to me and to a lot others too. Thanks for recommending my book, you know what I mean.

Charles Magaiza – I am humbled by your acceptance to guide and endorse my work. I find inspiration in your legacy of authorship. I want to be able to follow suit with God's help.

Bester Zambuko – Thanks for your support throughout this project. Who better to do the cover of my book than you? I am happy you did it, friends for life.

Mark Rushdoony - Thank you sir for permission to use your materials for my book.

Wycliff Chiunda – This would not be complete without mentioning the crucial role of editing this work. I could never ask for a better editor. Thank you for the hard work and many hours you dedicated to this work.

Rev Nyamakawo – My pastor, chief encourager, without your belief in me, I probably would have stopped midway. I am thoroughly blessed to be under your guidance. Thank you for the endorsement. Thank you for the prayers.

Let me single out a few individuals also who really inspired me and had unwavering belief in me. These people probably believed in me more than I did to my own self. This work owes its existence to you Tanya Pangeti and Rachel Sigola.

Omega Munyanyiwa, you are one reason, I kept writing. Thanks for the push, the book is finally here.

My two lovely daughters Unathi and Thandeka Kuwana, my greatest supporters, I derive inspiration from your unreserved belief in me. Yes, I am 'The Greatest Author in the World'. Let this book inspire you also.

My dear wife, Thobekile for your support and endurance. I am sorry for the many lonely nights, but I hope it was all worth it. Thanks for believing in me. I love you to the core. Let the world know.

Family - I am amazed at your faith in me. Mama and Daddy here are the results of your agonising hours of prayer for me.

To you all and those that I failed to mention by name, I love you all, please accept my heartfelt gratitude and pray that this book bears witness to the whole world.

Introduction

"Stop the Clock!" Is an exclamation? It is a call of desperation by someone who realises all of a sudden that time has overtaken them in life. It is like that moment when one wakes up and realises that his final exam starts in a few minutes. It is like that moment when you are caught up in a traffic jam and your wedding starts in 5 minutes. It is like that moment when the invigilator in an exam signals the end of the exam when you were right in the middle of giving your answer. It is like all such moments when you so desperately wish you could pause time just for a few moments. What is peculiar and agonising about this call is that it brings out an expression of regret, where one feels had they been granted thier wish their potential would have been realised and celebrated.

So that means anyone who finds themselves in such a situation has lost a chance to exercise and demonstrate their potential. The call "Stop the Clock!" is coming a little too late. The chance to show that potential at that very moment may be too difficult or impossible to rescue. However, if one could make that 'call', it would mean that potential which was yet to be released would still be stored somewhere in them. Making that "call awakens a new level of consciousness to time. Making that 'call' is an expression of a resolve of refusing to die while loaded with potential. "Stop the Clock!" is about realising what else you are about to lose if you do not wake up and collect yourself and become more alert when it comes to time.

Where ever you find yourself now, there is potential in you that is still to be released and realised. That is what this book is attempting to rescue. The first six chapters seek to find ways for individuals to develop a certain level of Time consciousness that causes discipline in the arena of time and therefore, triggers the achievement of extra ordinary results in life.

We stress the point that it is how you exploit your moments NOW that determines the brightness of your FUTURE. We also briefly address time as it pertains to business. We offer solutions that are basic but would make a big difference in your organisation if well considered. The next phase of the book shifts attention to discovering time.

We seek to understand why time behaves the way it does. We trace its origins to the beginning and what we believe to be its source and its beginning in a language that is basic and easy to comprehend. The idea in studying its behaviour in this manner is to have a thorough understanding and knowledge about it so that we equip ourselves to confront it better.

We failed to explain 'time' in any other way other than its source in God. We then chronicle how He got it to be and we study as to how He planned for time. From there we offer the prescriptions we borrow from Him. What better way to learn about a thing than to learn from its inventor? That is the attitude carried in this book. The last section deals with how God himself is willing to come in our defense as we struggle to harness and realign ourselves with time.

It gives a number of methods designed in our favour to equip us to face time and be confident as we confront it. It is my belief, that as you read this book your level of consciousness to this resource (time) shall increase and pull you out from a level where you feel comfortable with yourself to a level where you realise that every moment in life counts. It has taken years to come up with this book, but even after all that, I feel we have not exhausted the subject. During the long period I have taken to compile this work, I have certainly had a chance and privilege to test some of the concepts that I have recommended in this book in my own personal life, and I must encourage you by saying it is worth giving it a shot. Read, enjoy and transform your life.

Chapter 1
Time and Leadership

After a powerful and 'very' successful conference at my church, some few years ago, the committee which had been set up to organise the hosting of the conference re-grouped to evaluate the performance. I happened to be part of that team. Despite having been described as a wonderful event, a lot of administrative issues had, however, gone wrong. Some items on the programme had either been shifted, or cut short or at times even abandoned completely to compensate for slip ups on time during the course of the event. Imagine the embarrassment, when on one of the days, the main speaker, a guest preacher from a far-away land, where time is valued better(I guess) had to wait in his car, for us 'guests' to arrive. Being a time-conscious individual, he kept himself busy, while waiting, by reading a book which he had already targeted to clear in earnest.

In the meanwhile, I was still home. I stayed a few minutes' drive away from the venue. My pastor, as always, had already arrived and was beginning to feel the pressure. Surprisingly, on that day, almost everyone in the organizing team had been late and things stood still. He was to send text messages to every one of us. The text message was very brief. It did not even mention the word 'time' in it, or the word, 'late', or anything like that. It just simply had the exclamation, "LEADERS!!!" in capitals as shown here. Before I could open it, I only imagine the kind of tone and contents it carried. I hesitated and decided not to read it at that time, knowing where it was coming from, and of course why it was coming. Well, I had to anyway and when I eventually did, it simply confirmed my fears. So with that extra nudge, suddenly, I got into the time-conscious mode. Now, I had to drive everybody into the car for take-off. Being in 'the time conscious' mode, I took off for the venue showing my intention to make up for the lost time. I couldn't help noticing panic actions of my passengers. Just as soon as I had driven a few metres, I heard the clicking sounds of seatbelts being quickly secured and fastened everywhere in the car. I also noticed the person sitting on the front passenger's side of the car instinctively attempting to step on 'brakes.' They must have been imaginary though, because when I checked, I could not see any brakes that side, and besides; there has never brakes on that side of a right hand drive car anyway. At this point, let me warn the reader, that I am offering no prizes for guessing who that particular passenger was. So there is no incentive in doing that, if I were you. However, should curiosity get the better of you and you want to know, then; you have to read on a little further down the pages.

I had no intention to reveal that identity, but if you are still reading up to now, you probably deserve to know. So only for your sake, I shall reveal that later on in the book. So keep at it, you will certainly figure out or find out. Anyway, we managed to get to the venue 'safely'. When I got to church, I thought I was just going to sneak in unnoticed and disappear into the crowd, but as fate would have it, a key member of the musical group was also late. Coincidentally, that happened to be my area of responsibility during that conference. The pastor was on the look-out for anyone who was to arrive first and deal with this situation also. So I walked straight into his face in shame (of-course) and face down, as he stood in the foyer leading to the main auditorium. As you might know, the one who arrives on time for a function, seems to wields some kind of authority over the one who comes late, no matter the status of either person. I have observed this phenomenon many times over, and it seems to hold true always. Just take a minute and reflect for a moment that time when you got to a venue late and had been expected to deliver a service.

What feelings did you experience as you prepared to face those who had already arrived before you? Did you just walk there with a straight face and felt no feelings of guilt? No sign of anxiety? No worry? No uneasiness? No concern? No temptation to lie, etc.?

If you answered 'no' to these questions, then it means your time consciousness is still very much alive and expresses an inward desire to make amends. Something can be done to improve it. One or more of the above negative feelings, is bound to flow through you during such situations. It is this flow of these negative emotions that 'belittles' you and causes you to submit to the better time keepers. That temporary experience you go through from the time 'your service' starts being demanded for, and yet you are still not there to render it, is quite significant, because it forms the basis of our first law of time.

The law of time conferred authority.
Time gives temporary authority to the one who is in harmony with it, over the one who is not.

Mark this, if you make it on time for any event and others or some fail; at the point of contact with them at that event, no matter who you are, whatever your position, you will have placed yourself in a position of authority over them. Accept it, or not, that is the reality. The significance of this law is validated by the flow of negative emotions which one experiences and is triggered by the thoughts that run wild in your mind, when late or when you fail to make it on time.

Can you recall one incident where you were late for an important engagement? What thoughts ran through your mind as you made you way to the venue? Did you think about crafting a believable and convincing story to justify your lateness? Did you think of a time wasting detour you made earlier? Did you keep thinking about the consequences of your lateness? For instance, has the meeting started in my absence? So who took my place of taking the minutes of the meeting, etc. These thoughts invariably trigger certain emotions that then run through you. You begin to experience negative emotions like anxiety, regret, frustration, guilt, feeling pressured, depressed, etc. In that state; your positive self- image is bruised, and negativity, is amplified.

If this process keeps repeating itself, it will eventually confirm your failure. It is important to specifically single out 'time' as the predominant cause of the flow of these negative emotions. If for example the actors in the 'cast' were to switch roles, always the one who plays 'the late comer's role will be the one to experience these negative emotions, and consequently, become subject to the better time keeper. The danger though of being a habitual poor time keeper, is the guaranteed occurrence of the process which dampens your self-worth, and consequently, the repeated experience of this negative energy each time an incident involving time occurs. It means, instead of always experiencing the positive emotions as listed in Table 1 below.

Positive Human Emotions

Gladness	Hopeful	able	adequate	happiness
Expectation	Optimistic	capable	confident	great
Delighted	Relieved	Joyful	satisfaction	strong
Thrilled	Certain	sublime	powerful	Exhilarated
Comfortable	Eager	stable	interested	love
Relaxed	surprised	positive	fascinated	compassion
Pleasant	excited	exceptional	awe	sympathy
Peaceful	Lively	magnificent	inspired	empathy
Contented	enthusiastic	unique	glorious	affirmative

Table 1

You inevitably find yourself engrossed in negative energy reflected in the emotions listed in Table 2.

Negative Human Emotions

jealousy	bitterness	spitefulness	nervousness	uncomfortable
manipulative	worrisome	repulsive	timidity	annoyance
pressured	Anxiety	embarrassment	apprehensive	frustrated
Regret	Stressed	envious	hostile	guilt
overwhelmed	exasperated	destructive	greedy	helplessness

Table 2

What Happens when a leader shows disregard for time?

Research has proven that negative emotions experienced by a person, are potentially harmful to the owner of the feelings and have a negative effect on the well-being of others around them. The status of emotional wellness is a quality that is desirable in any human being, but how much more so for a person in leadership. A leader, who is consistently in this state, fortifies his position and endorses his leadership and authority as often as he does so. A leader who strives to achieve and maintain this emotional state always, makes an unequivocal public declaration of his intention to remain a leader. In this 'frame', the leader exhibits qualities that confirm his leadership, and defends his integrity by displaying his willingness and ability to:

1. *"Live and work independently while realizing the importance of seeking and appreciating the support and assistance of others."*

    This is important because managers or leaders are meant to be paid or rewarded for results they achieve through others, even though they could have achieved the same results by their own effort.

2. *"Form interdependent relationships with others based upon a foundation of mutual commitment, trust and respect."*

Managers depend on their ability to influence relationships in pursuance of their goals and creating an environment which promotes mutual support and mutually beneficial relationships.

3. "Take on challenges, take risks, and recognise conflict as being potentially healthy."

Managers should have the confidence to lead and be able to resolve conflict with subordinates as well as resolve conflict between them. This confidence is made possible by their effort to maintain influence over the subordinates.

4. "Manage your life in personally rewarding ways, and taking responsibility for your actions."

Good Managers take charge of their actions and are personally responsible for their achievements and acknowledge their mistakes.

All the above are qualities of a good and esteemed leader. Now imagine the effect on all these qualities, on a leader who has been repeatedly subjected to negative emotions as listed above, by their habit of being late and who by this act keep compromising their integrity. Take note that these emotions are an automatic response and their effect on the mind of the person is real and each time this happens; it confirms and strengthens his failure as a leader. His leadership status is weakened. Time has a lot to do with Leadership.

Wellness quotations numbered 1-4 on this page taken and adapted from wellness.ucr.edu>URC Home>Human Resurces>welness

The Flow of Negative Emotions

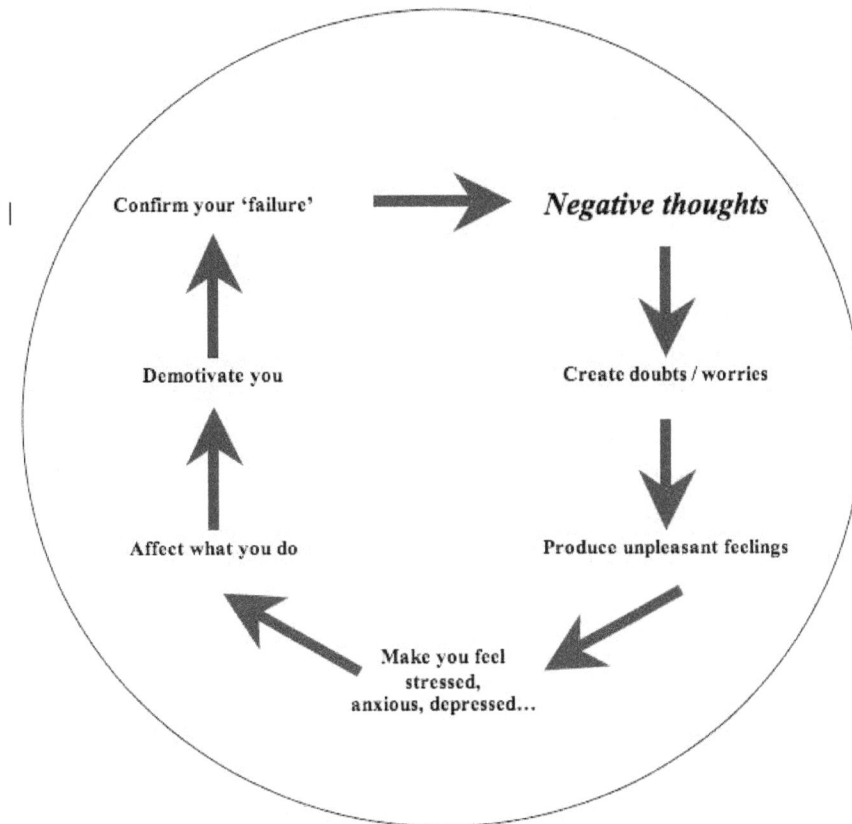

Figure 1

That's why it is important for leaders to have a high degree of respect for time or else risk compromising their authority and in the process also compromising the organisation's culture, if it has time values. Imagine what happens if the above scenario repeats itself for long enough, say in a church set up. It eventually establishes a 'parallel' authority in the system at the subconscious level, and strengthened by a repeated incident. So in essence, what this means is that at the conscious level, there exists the human conferred authority (the leadership as we know it) and at the sub conscious level, another form of leadership.

(Diagram adapted from The Vicious Circle of Negative Automatic Thinking-iveronicawalsh.worldpress.com)

The 'Time conferred leadership'. It has often been said that; what we can't see in this world, is far more powerful than anything we can see.' Well fortunately, this statement can be taken as being subjective. But I can safely assert that if this 'leadership crisis' is not resolved by the leaders themselves, taking concrete action to correcting and reclaiming their full responsibility and authority, no matter what action, you employ to improve time management efforts in this setup, be it in church, business, organisation, etc; you are merely wasting more of your time. If it is important enough, leaders should lead, and the rest will follow their leaders.

The risk of the organisation not taking action at the first notice of such pattern is that of 'culture decay'. This will spread like a cancer in the whole organisation. Remember a leader exerts his influence upon his followers. All the efforts and 'time inspired values' or beliefs if any, held by the organisation are under threat from such behaviour from leaders. What makes it regrettable is the fact that, it is the leadership which is unconsciously destroying what they consciously wish to enforce.

Chapter 2

The Transitional Phases (Times) of life.

Now, back to our earlier but unfinished story, I am sure we have made our point on leadership. So it was now about 20 minutes after the scheduled starting time. The Pastor did not even pass a comment concerning my coming late, but his disappointment was written all over his face. Of-course this incident and the negative energy that I felt during the whole drama, was enough motivation for me to consciously make up my mind to try not to disappoint on the remaining days of the conference. Guess what? I managed, and so did all my other colleagues and 'partners in crime'. The surprising thing though was that, the sooner had the conference ended, the sooner did we all forget and let the old habit kick in again. I guess the old adage is so right after all, "old habits die hard." Now that I look at it, it's simple to appreciate why. The culture of respecting time was just simply not there. It takes deliberate effort to build and sustain such a culture. There was just not enough motivation to drive sustained time consciousness. If at one time it was there, over the years, it must have been replaced by a culture that gave no notice of time inspired values.

So as we sat there, in the chill of the night, reviewing the conference, everyone spoke about everything else with so much passion and zeal and came up with commendable strategies to correct the shortcomings for better future events. As far as I can recall, though, there was no satisfactory strategy mooted to correct shortcomings evident on the management of time during that event, well at least according to me. In-fact the best contribution, to that effect, was a passionate appeal from the pastor, for members to try to be more time conscious. At least, he had a moral standing to make that appeal, remember he never came late the entire conference. He had full authority to make that call, derived first from his leadership role as pastor, and then secondly from the 'time' conferred authority. This was about as much as was offered at that review, as a solution and strategy for the thing that almost threatened to spoil the conference.

This particular incident got me thinking. I had many thoughts and questions running in my mind. Did we do enough to address the issue to avoid a repeat? Why is time so difficult to keep anyway? What is it that we call 'time'? Is it spiritual? Do we have control over it? How did it come to be and when? Is there a way it can be stopped etc? These questions lingered in my mind and that was sufficient to prompt me, coupled with personal experiences and encounters with it, to attempt exploring of this subject further. To me, though passionate, the appeal made by the pastor was not enough, to effect a sustained change in the people's behaviour within the organisation. At best, it might have just moved a few individuals to awaken to their consciousness for as long as it took them to remember. To this day, time issues still remain a big challenge at the church. A few piecemeal tactics keep being implemented to try managing this resource, but in my opinion, a more comprehensive new culture has to be developed.

The leadership has to acknowledge firstly the existence of this scenario and secondly, agree to classify it as a problem affecting the efficiency of the organisation, and thirdly, be in agreement to change that situation and lastly and even more importantly, commit to making that change happen. I should warn that this decision is not a stroll in the park. It is a decision that would affect even the lives of members outside the activities of the organisation. Comfort zones will be interfered with, and the question is; how many are willing to get out of their comfort zones? For corporate, it may not be as difficult to enforce as people do not have much of a choice. This is a perfect example where a series of training workshops etc have to be conducted for members to acquire relevant education. It may be helpful to enlist services of a change agent in the process, because this is not normally regarded as an area where people can receive training.
It is the hope of the author, that by the time one gets to end of this of book, the reader will be able to regard the whole subject of time as an area where one can receive as well as give training to improve on its usage. The first obstacle in confronting and dealing with this matter is procrastination. Do not delay confronting it. Start right away, there is no such thing as a 'perfect' time to start on anything. How well is time being managed in your area? It should concern you in the first instance, because it also affects your personal time management.

On my own person, dealing with 'time' in virtually all spheres of life, has also been a great challenge. In most cases the result of my interaction with time and its management has been failure to manage it properly. In fact, let me confess that the greatest inspiration in coming up with this work, has been as a result of a deep introspection from within. This was in an attempt to deal with those shortcomings in mastering own time and in pursuing a fulfilled life. In the process, this would impact on the life of others around me and inspire them to 'improve' their own. The way I have so badly fared in this area, qualifies me as a good candidate to be writer of such a book, as they say 'experience is the best teacher'. The story above is just a tip of the ice-burg in the said experience. I would not know the extent to which you, the reader relate, or how much you identify with some or all of the above.

As I began on this journey of trying to understand 'time', I made some very intriguing findings about the phases of life that we all pass through. It was a wakeup call for me and this made me realise more of the value of time to my existence on earth. We pass through various phases in our lifetime, with each phase characterised by a natural lack of one or more of very key resources of life; namely money, time or energy. These are illustrated in the Table 3 below for clarity.

It is most important to note that the age group classification given in the table is subjective and only meant as a guide and in no way meant to stereotype or pass any form of judgement on any particular class of people.

The writer is aware that people are different and may not necessarily be limited to behaviours or traits listed under the said categories. There are no hard-and- fast rules on this one. In one of the chapters to come, we discuss 'chance'. We acknowledge that chance has no regard for logic, when it happens to you, it defies the norm. For instance, a 32 years-old intelligent man may find himself having covered all this in a few years, what would ordinarily take several years for an ordinary man. In that case, where others are crying for having lost ground on time, he has, in fact, gained time, and it would be difficult to class him in the general way. So in coming up with this table, the writer is merely giving guidelines based on what is generally accepted as standard and the table is a generalised view. Each person is encouraged to come up with one that more accurately represents their situation but following the broad framework provided in the table.

Behaviours exhibited at different stages of life

Stage in Life	First 30 years of life	Next 40 years	70+ years
Scarcest resource in each stage	Money	Time	Energy
Opportunity for exploiting time	Abundant supply of time Appreciation of value and opportunity is remote	Pressure mounts for time as reality of approaching stage dawns, value of time soars	Limited opportunity No price tag can be placed on time
Stage Behaviour towards time	Little appreciation of value Inadvertently Too much waste Procrastination is rife	Value realisation Consciousness at its peak Battle with Procrastination	Desperate for realised value Regret Always wish they had done much earlier.
Response to time pressures	Volunteer their time to those who now know better Quite generous	Tend to buy time from those wasting it Want conserve every little bit of time left	Would pay anything to have it Seeking where to find it
Stage Attitude	There is still time I shall do it later, let it pass for now. ☺	Hey! Where did all the time go to? There is no more time to do everything now! I will do what I can ☺	I can still do it all the same. ☹ ؟
Workload passed to future ☞	Passed to next age group ☞☞☞☞☞	Burden too overwhelming passed to next age ☞☞☞☞☞	Can't cope, all the difficult work left for this stage

Cont…

☺	☺	☺	☺
Blame for wasted time passed backwards from the future 🕊	Why is everyone blaming me?	This guy should have done this surely. 🕊🕊🕊	What lazy blokes!!! 🕊🕊🕊 Everything left for me to do.

Table 3

Don't Sabotage yourself

Instant gratification is sweet, but brings sour results with time. The 'now' moment, in reality, does not exist, because the moment you become aware of it; it has already moved into the realm of past time. Now is a moving target if I may say so. It flows from the future to the past. It is elusive. The past and the future are more authentic, but of the two, the future should be your overriding priority. It is the only period left, that you can be sure to live in, and have the power now to change it, to what you desire. That picture you see of your desired future should start forming in your mind, now. That is the intended job of 'now'. Many people seem to fail to set right their priorities and take full advantage of and maximise their potential during the requisite phases of life. It's amazing how, suddenly some find themselves having arrived in their last phase and faced with hard facts. The opportunity for time will be gone; the optimum opportunity for making money will be gone and energy levels now at their lowest. It is late, no matter the amount of willpower, the signs that indicate the scarcity of time at that age will confirm that truth. At the time, the young person was busy passing or shifting the work load to the next phase of life; he was, in fact, performing acts of self-sabotage. All that work that arose during his youthful age should have been dealt with at that time. That was the most appropriate time for performing those tasks.

I was also deeply moved to share the thoughts in this book with the young to urge them to jealously guard this most prized possession in their hands and avoid the mistake of falling in the same trap as their predecessors, who are now old. As Jonathan Edwards puts it in his sermon, 'The preciousness of time' "The first of a man's time, after he comes to the exercise of his reason, and to be capable of performing his work, is the best." It should be made known to every young person that they are at the prime of their time and should make the best use of it. Every one of them should become conscious of this fact, and to know that time is an opportunity. If I be allowed, may I labour a bit on this point, because I feel it is a point worth driving home?

Dictionary.com gives a definition that I like and would wish to use. It says opportunity is "a situation or condition favourable for the attainment of a goal" and young people should be made aware that, that situation or condition which promotes the attainment of goals in a person's life is what they possess, right now! So while at that age, 'time' is an opportunity, at another age time becomes something else, certainly not an opportunity, and that's why any class of people past that age, would value it as priceless and pay any price for that opportunity.

I have an ex-boss, who used to say, "Young Lavhu! (a shortened corruption of my name) Do you know that being young is an asset?" I never forgot those words, and they kept inspiring and influencing my life. I became conscious of those words to this day, and made decisions in life based on that valuable advice. I always wish every young person knew what assets, they are, which every elderly person would pay any amount to possess. When they pay you lots of money at your workplace, they are buying your opportunity, and that's why business employs the young. How much do you value your opportunity? Time is an opportunity, young man!

So, let the author make this declaration, this day, that "I am no master of time myself, neither have I lived a life that bears the greatest testimony to a life that has conquered and defeated time, but the greatest assurance I want to give the reader, is that by the time I finish this book, my own life is going to turn a new leaf. After this work, it's not possible to remain with the same attitude towards 'time' in any sphere of my life" If this book can't challenge and deal decisively with the author's own life, concerning the 'improvement' of his own time on earth, then, what good is it to any-body? In-fact, the author should emerge as the biggest beneficiary of this 'piece of work'. So be assured reader, please read on, even the author can't wait to learn. That's how confident I am about the impact of this book upon your life. In the next chapter, I would like to draw lessons from the above story.

Exercise

1. From today, begin to take steps to stop the habit of arriving late for anything. Start by establishing the purpose of taking that action, and work to fulfill that purpose.

2. Come up with your own slogan, which encourages you to act now and not let things pass to your future. Memorise that phrase and vocalise it, every day. Get into the habit of chanting your own slogan each time there is the temptation to procrastinate on crucial matters.

3. Identify the phase in which you are and assess your performance against the general standard suggested in the table. How do you fare? What are you going to do starting today to change which ever attribute you feel deserves remedial attention?

Chapter 3
The cost of lost time

Let me start by citing Jonathan Edwards again from the same sermon quoted earlier, he says – "indeed, our welfare in this world depends upon its improvement. If we improve it not, we shall be in danger of coming to poverty and disgrace; however, by a good improvement of it, we may obtain those things, which will be useful and comfortable. However, it is above all things precious, as our state through eternity depends upon it. The importance of the improvement of time upon other accounts is in subordination to this. Thus if a man, by anything he hath, may save his life, which he must lose without it, he will look upon that by which he hath the opportunity of escaping so great an evil as death, to be very precious.

In the previous chapter, we learnt that 'time' affords us an 'opportunity' to escape a poor-quality life on earth. From the quotation above, we also learn of another opportunity, a 'superior' one as it seems, this time affording us the opportunity to escape eternal misery. We shall not discuss it at this time, but with this newly suggested opportunity, it should be in our best interest, to talk about it at some point. Keep the thought in mind as we shall come back to it later.

For the time being, we continue with the idea of time being an opportunity for a better quality of life during our time on earth. I have observe that 'time' operates within a well thought-out 'system' which is highly repetitive, and it is disciplined enough to obey the rules of that system, at whatever cost. We can certainly predict its presence and behaviour in the future based on its consistent past. In other words, its pattern has been and remains very obvious. It just does what it was instructed and fashioned to do. It keeps going, and you can predict that tomorrow it shall be going, a year later nothing will have changed; and even beyond that it shall still be going! This is an attribute which 'time' has displayed over many,

many past centuries and this has inspired a thought in me. If this is the behaviour of time, and it is this predictable, then why don't I take advantage of this pattern and plan for my time? Not only just plan for my time now, but even plan well into the future.

In fact, what would stop me from making a (time) budget for my entire life? I can develop short term plans, and still budget my time for the long term based on this known behaviour. But why should I make such a suggestion? Well, I should think it is simple. As the clock ticks away, so does my life. As the clock ticks away, so does the energy within me. I am sure of the fact that, for as long as the clock ticks, it is a reminder of where life is taking me. I cannot afford to continue to be shrouded in confusion and keep losing more precious time. So if one has to contend and not be overwhelmed by it, they should consider planning for it, both for the present while there is still some energy in one's being, as well as in the future when the energy of life starts diminishing. In doing so, the plan should take into account, the changing circumstances of life that come with each tick of the clock and appropriately allocate the time. This is like suggesting that one should develop a 'strategic plan' for their lives. Sounds like business now, doesn't it? However, yes, in a way, that's what this is all about. To be blunt, yes, develop a strategic plan for your life, the same way you craft one for your businesses. Isn't it ironic, how our business lives seem better planned for than our own personal lives? Doing this will certainly assist us better manage the time that was allocated to our individual lives.

This book shall try and address both these areas of our lives, and so it is important to note that the suggestions offered here are also applicable at corporate level. We shall, wherever possible throughout the book try to show the distinction between corporate matters and personal issues.

From the story relayed in the earlier chapter, another piece of information that had been withheld from you was that the conference had to be extended by another day, to make use of the main speaker, as he had missed his plane and had to extend his stay with the church for a few more days. Organisers of his travel arrangements also slipped up. I include this detail at this point, not to show a total collapse of time management at the church, but rather to stress the point that time obeys its instruction at whatever cost. This attribute of time deserves special human attention, as disregarding it would create cost centres in the lives of people. This would be the same even for business. The moment we just slip up and let time tick away; a cost is created and hangs over our shoulders. In other words, humans have to come up with a response to this attribute of time to limit the cost that it would bring. What that means, in essence, is that a human being has to attempt to become conscious of every single moment that passes in their lives and guards it jealously if they were to reduce the effects of the cost of lost time. Now, how achievable is this task? I would say, it is almost an impossible task. Surely our desire to be attentive can never match the pulse of time. We can only be conscious of time and tracking it for so long, thereafter; it overtakes us and goes into some dimension of wasted, or unmanaged, or unnoticed, or unaccounted for time, and therein lies the various losses associated with time. The cost we incur as a result comes in various forms, including monetary losses, emotional losses, etc. For those that can be quantified, we quantify them and translate that into monetary value, because it is the measure to which we can assign a value and can quickly come to an understanding of the magnitude of our losses. However, time can also be lost and the costs incurred and the circumstances may be difficult to quantify because one cannot place money value on the loss.

For example, time lost when a man dates a woman and never gets to commit to marrying her until the relationship fails. It is a painful loss, not because one cannot afford to find another person to be with, but the investment in time that was committed to the relationship which probably happened during the prime of one's time. This would have translated into negative results for the future for one party and lost opportunity, where one would have invested that time in perhaps a more fruitful relationship.

The cost borne by the person in this scenario, is the 'opportunity cost'. What productive thing could they have done with all that time gone to waste? However, in all these incidences, we realize that time respects no one, it is not moved by circumstances, it is not controlled by emotions. If it was controlled by such or any other consideration, it probably would have stopped for a moment to allow the man of God to catch his plane. It might have stopped as well for that lady whose time was wasted, but alas; it doesn't wait. In all these circumstances, time will still pass on like as if nothing had changed and all we are left to do is count the losses, leading us to our second law of time.

The law of opportunity

Any moment you encounter in time, is pregnant with potential and opportunity.

Any wasted time or time not well managed or time that cannot be accounted for, always come at a cost and the cost stems from the facts inherent in this law. It doesn't really matter the cause of the wastage, as long as time has been lost, a cost is attached, often times quantifiable in monetary value. An individual, for instance, can cost the whole organisation thousands of dollars by a simple act of deciding to turn a blind eye to the clock at a crucial moment.

The lady, who could not secure the marriage she had hoped for after investing her time in the relationship, suffered loss and now has to contend with the "cost" of the failed relationship, even though she did not cause the waste. So, it's simple, people we interact with and allow in our time-space are potential causes of this "cost". This brings a sad reality of life that we have to accept, that it is not possible to exploit all opportunities that time brings to us. Some will certainly slip out of our hands, either through our own doing or even the doing of others.

The opportunity carried in that moment will have been lost. As long as it stays within our means to control, time remains an opportunity, and on the other side, we begin to count the cost of that opportunity. We should plug such leaks by placing good stewards in our institutions and also be selective on those we allow to affect our time in order to protect our opportunity. I have known businesses to be aggressive when it comes to protecting their opportunities. Why should the opportunities presented by time to an individual's life be treated any different? They too should be guarded and fortified. If all businesses took this statement with the seriousness, it would deserve, they would surely change their perspective and approach towards how they value time in their organisations. They would invest to safeguard this resource, the same way they would craft systems to safe guard their cash. The cash they protect so much, is to a greater extent a result of well managed time. I want to throw a challenge to business leaders and managers; your organisation would be worth much more today if you exerted just a little more effort in recognising and managing time as a real resource of the company. It's understandable though as to why time management is not regarded a priority.

This is because time is the only resource that the company exploits without spending a cent on acquiring it, but it is also by far the most expensive resource held by companies. An organisation is as profitable as its time was exploited in production. On the other hand, an individual is as developed to the extent of his exploited time. Employ resources to maximise your opportunity. In the coming chapters, I shall suggest some tactics that can be useful in exploiting the potential locked in time, both in the life of individuals and that of companies. For the individual, it is important to point out though that the strategies we suggest here do not operate in isolation. Two key conditions have to have been fulfilled in order for them to be completely effective.

Employ them in the context of 'a life-long budget' for your time

In other words, have a time plan that covers your entire life. However, this is not possible if something else very crucial is not defined in your life, and we believe it is a fundamental aspect that has to be addressed by every individual, – it is called purpose.

Strive to know your purpose

If purpose is known, then setting of a life-long plan for your time becomes a workable idea. It helps you give priority to activities that support your destination. Your allocation of time to tasks in your budget becomes guided by it. We shall look at both these aspects in greater detail later in the book, for now we have laid enough foundation to enable clear comprehension of the fundamentals discussed in the next chapter.

Exercise:

1. Take time to think hard about your purpose. Do you have a purpose? If you do, do you already know what it is? This is very important if the rest of our discussion is going to be of benefit to you.

2. If you don't know your purpose, why don't you start today to take action to discover what it is? Living outside your purpose is playing injustice to your "time". Start the journey of discovering your purpose today.

Chapter 4
Develop a time-conscious Mind

As I was writing this book, I was also drawn into growing my faith in the idea of natural laws that govern life in the universe. The most striking one to me, and which I have started practicing is; The law of Attraction. It is a law to the effect that, whatever dominates your thoughts, is that same thing, you shall attract into your life. Because it is a law, whether you know about it, or you don't, it will still affect you. Personally, I would think it is better to have such knowledge, than to be affected by what you don't know. And because it is a law, it means; it applies to you as much as it does to me and everybody else. As I have come to understand it now, this law is in operation in your life even right now as you read this book. Take a moment to reflect. What thoughts dominated your mind today or even now and then reconcile this with your experiences for the day? Do you see what you spent the day creating and attracting to yourself? Keep tracking your thoughts from today and observe the results. Whatever result you get from this, consider taking action. Either maintain your thought patterns, if it is attracting good thoughts for you, or change it to shape your desired life.

Now, if thoughts are that powerful, that they can create the reality of my life, can I not use them as a weapon to counter the strong traits that time uses against me? As we shall learn in chapters that follow, time has a beginning, and from that instant, it has never receded. It has never stopped at any instant, and it is likely never to. This is the consistency of the thing we seek to battle. So in terms of experience, consistency and tenacity, time is far ahead of us. Any person, that works on possessing these attributes positions themselves for a disciplined life that stands a better chance with time. Our minds are the most powerful weapons we can use to fight our battle with anything in life, including time. My research pointed me towards the sub-conscious mind. We all possess this thing. I was astounded to discover that, this is the thing that 'creates' your life. What is written in your subconscious mind is what your reality is or will be! IT IS IMPOSSIBLE TO BE ANY OTHER WAY. The belief held by your subconscious mind holds true and manifests itself in the physical always. For example, you cannot believe you are rich and be poor. You cannot believe you have a sharp memory, and be forgetful. Your true self lies in the subconscious mind. The experiences you went through, what you saw, and what you heard about time all contributed to the programming that you received in that arena, and which now controls your behaviour and your automatic responses to the outside world pertaining to time. Just as those past experiences were responsible for your programming, it is also possible to create conditions that can re-programme your mind in order to change the course in any area of your life, time included. Any kind of change in one's behaviour or attitude is impossible without first changing what is sitting in your subconscious mind.

Exercise:
Examine your Time Consciousness

Take a moment to reflect on how you have made use of your time to this day. Ponder on these questions and assess your Time consciousness.

1.   What beliefs do you hold about time?
2.   How are those beliefs affecting how you handle your   time?
3.   Do you believe that time is important?
4.   What steps have you taken in life to reflect how important time is in your life?
5.   Do you find it important to plan for your time?
6.   Does it appeal to you to manage or have a system of planning for your time?
7   Have you ever taken time to set up a programme to help you manage time?
8.   Do you own a watch?
9.   Does it appeal to you to have a life-long plan for your time?

10. Do you believe that your life would have been at a better stage by now, had you known better about time earlier?

11. Do you believe that unmanaged time, unaccounted for time, unnoticed time, unplanned times are all sources of high 'costs' to your life?

12. Have you always failed to finish an exam because you were slow?

13. Have you always had to apologise for being late to the extent that your apology loses meaning, and you are no longer taken seriously by colleagues?

14. Do you find it comfortable getting to an event late no matter what event it is?

15. Do you remember the last time you were early for anything at all?

16. Do you find yourself late even when it seemed obvious you would make it on time?

17. If you are a leader, do you find it normal when your subordinates arrive late for work?

18. Does it ever occur to you that you are already out of time?

19. Do you also acknowledge that all the above are ills that can be corrected?

I could go on and on and on asking these questions. I don't know how you were programmed, and how you responded to all those questions. However, your true and honest responses to these questions reflect your programming in the area of time. You may need to take action starting today to change the way you behave towards time and improve your awareness.

You can never be truly successful in any human endeavor if your time programming is wrong. You can never succeed in being time conscious unless this programming is corrected.

So your programming and the need for its reprogramming, was the first basis upon which we recommend that you cooperate with your mind to deal better with issues pertaining to your time. The second and equally important reason is its (mind) overriding responsibility of making life possible. It is (the sub conscious mind) responsible for controlling critical processes in the body, like your heartbeat, your breathing, your digestion, etc. These are aspects that if you had to think about, in order to perform them, you would surely struggle to keep up with the demand for the concentration required. Just imagine if you had to think that now it's time for the next breath, and the next and the next and so on. Or to say I now need to cause the next heart beat and the next and the next. Imagine the chaos.

The subconscious mind does all this without you consciously thinking about it. It is genetically programmed to perform those tasks, and it does so without effort. I don't know about you, but I seem to have discovered in the mind, a weapon almost equal to the way time operates. If we had a way of reprogramming our subconscious mind with good time values and attitudes, and we let it take over the responsibility of managing our responses to time issues, don't you think we would never ever have to struggle with time again? A befitting example in this scenario is your sleeping and wake-up time. The subconscious mind is responsible for reminding you that it's now time to wake up, even though you are fast asleep, or even when having a good dream, the mind will make sure you wake up exactly the time you always do. Except of course when there is a special cause. You don't need to set an alarm. When it's time up, it's time up.
The mind will make sure the message has been relayed.

Drive time consciousness promoting values into your mind through repetition

The good thing worth celebrating about programming your mind, is that, no matter what retrogressive values you hold on a subject, in this case, time, if you should decide and commit to changing them, the mind will accept that change. It's a process certainly, and will require dedication and a lot of patience with yourself to achieve the objective. So definitely, what you have been programmed to think concerning any subject in life, can be reversed or changed if you make a conscious decision to do so. It's not a permanent damage if your mind was wrongly programmed, and it's usually the case, because you are not entirely in control of this process. A lot of factors, most of them beyond your control went into influencing the way your subconscious mind was set.

You can re-align your thoughts and condition your mind anew, replacing old and counter-productive values with good and efficient ones. Once you settle and are confident of the content you wish to 'upgrade' your mind with, you can begin the process. Engaging into repetitive activities meant to assist in this effort is one of the most well accepted methods of learning. The ultimate objective of the process is to make the activity a stored routine in the mind. If repeated action is pursued long enough it becomes a natural way of forcing the activity from the conscious level of the mind where deliberate action is being taken to develop the skill, to the sub conscious level, where it becomes permanently stored in a retrieval system and become an involuntary response when needed.

Let us consider a quick practical application of this concept. Let us assume that as you grew up, it was never impressed upon you; the value of an early start to your day.

That means subconsciously you do not believe it is important. You attend one of our seminars and get convinced that indeed it is a good habit, and that you currently lack and would wish to change that. You draw up a daily programme to help you achieve this objective. You will notice that as you begin the process, you even refer to the written instructions and with your mind being on full alert. With repeated action everyday it becomes less and less important to refer to your manual, and you begin to take the instruction from your mind. As you continue with the daily routine, your mind will eventually take over and automatically dictate responses to all situations that test this aspect of your life. For instance, it becomes an automatic practice retiring early; your body begins to reject further sleep past your wake- up time, your motivation and drive to start and accomplish tasks are normally high, etc. All these are responses of the mind in support of your stored values.

It is however, beyond the scope of this book to fully address the processes involved in reprogramming the mind to an alert and time-conscious mind. It takes a lot of training and discipline to achieve this. We shall however make all efforts possible to include information on our website that would be able to assist your effort in this regard, but here I only give enough information to stimulate the desire and initiate the process.

Making declarations of good Time Beliefs or Values to drive them into your mind

Another very effective way of charging and motivating yourself in achieving your goal of being conscious to time is by making declarations and affirmations about your time consciousness and the values that you wish to embrace. Declarations send strong messages of intent to the atmosphere, to you and to your mind. If done faithfully, consistently and correctly declarations produce magical results. Declarations are used in combination with repetitive action as discussed earlier, and the result is remarkable.

The more you declare that you respect time, and the more you make that declaration, the more it becomes a reality in your life. As long as you are passionate with your declarations, you are becoming what you will have wished for. Keep making these declarations. It is possible to change the programming of your mind and train it on a new path through declarations. The result of making declarations is the enrichment of the inside which would then manifest on the outside. That is why the ills that are time related in one's life, even at corporate level, are difficult to correct or resolve by just expressing intention or just sitting down and agreeing to a meeting that we need to become more time conscious. When something is driven from the inside, it is more powerful than something that has no permanent driver.

Trigger your Time Consciousness with associated representations

Some years ago, in the mid 1980's when I was in my third grade, I had a friend whom I truly admired and wished so badly to be like him. He was sharp in class, good at so many other things, well groomed, admired by all the girls in the class, always attracting good comments from teachers, etc. He had all the qualities a person of that age would admire. Now among those things which I admired about him was a unique scent that he carried on him. I vividly remember that scent even now as I write this I am ready to smell it. He also came from a background that could afford a bit of luxuries, which most of us could not at that time. And so at that age, he stood out as the only child to wear a perfume to school. The moment anybody would smell it, even without looking, they could tell he was nearby. It was more so for me, as he used to sit next to me in class.

So what has this got to do with time? Somebody might be asking. I would not blame you for asking, in-fact if you did, it would have shown that you were following the argument. Up to now, one would have struggled to figure out the connection.

However, let's decode the story anyway. As I narrated the story, I admitted that even now as I think about it, I am able to recall vividly the scent of my friend's perfume. If one was to alter it a bit, I am sure I would have been able to detect that change to the scent somehow. Amazingly, that fragrance, like many others, has stood the test of time, and still exists to this day. I often meet up with it in the corridors all over town. And this is where my story is. Over 30 years after, every time that I sense that scent, I think of that yesteryear friend. I don't have to struggle remembering it, for it comes as a natural instinct. The scent is a trigger that causes me to think of my friend. So I believe that if I buy that perfume and keep it in my room, I will be able to think about him each time that scent escapes from its bottle. I don't know what you think about that. Have you ever had that experience where the occurrence of something, draws you into a certain state or feeling or reminds you of a certain thing or incident? I have seen people who are drawn into a state of bliss when a specific song or music is played, and some who are drawn into sadness by the sounding of a drum sounding a certain way. Others have their mind jogged into to remembering to take their daily medication each time the first message signal sounds on their phones.

The reason as to why certain things are able to trigger various emotional states in us is because we had sometime in the past made an association between the two things. This association is then registered and stored in our subconscious mind, and becomes an automatic response once conditions for the association are achieved. This process of forming 'associations' in our everyday life occurs naturally in humans and is a continuous happening in life. Every state of 'being' that we experience in life, whether it be a feeling of being happy, or a state of being sad; or a state of being forgetful, or a state of being energised; or experiencing stage fright or even a display of confidence, or any other state for that matter, including also, being in a state of being Time Conscious has an experience or memory associated with it. Thus if you can trigger the elements that are associated with any particular state of your being, you will experience right at that moment that very state.

Your time consciousness can also be triggered in the very same way. I did say earlier that these 'associations' occur naturally, but the mind of a person can also be taught to consciously shape these 'associations.' And it is these that we seek to develop here by relating to this story. With constant practice and repetition, they (associated triggers) become firmly rooted in our minds. We can take advantage of building these new 'associations' to enhance our time awareness or consciousness. As an example, you could start by buying a wrist watch and start working with your mind to build an 'association' between it and your time consciousness. The watch triggers you to remain time conscious each time you have sight of it; it becomes a trigger and causes you to become conscious of time, and so you act accordingly. So anytime you see the watch, you are reminded, that time is important and that wasted time comes with a cost, that being late for an event, puts others in a place of advantage over you, that if you know your purpose, you can have a lifelong plan for your time, etc., and you immediately adjust your actions to respond to the message conveyed by sight of the watch. So no matter what situation you find yourself in, the sight of the watch just triggers an involuntary response which supports your desire to take charge of your time. The association between the watch and your alertness to time is established and can even be made stronger by your continued effort to promote it. Repeated action and respecting the 'association' and what it stands for is what you have to commit to doing.

Do not leave anything to chance; strengthen this practice by having as many symbols or items of this association as possible, so that there are more symbols to remind you to keep your 'time' attitude. You can form these associations with symbols, music, posters, slogans,   items, etc. whatever you choose to use, as long as it carries value that you personally respect and would be compelled into action by it.

Confront and deal with forgetfulness and inattention.

One of the silent killers of time is forgetfulness. It is widely accepted that as one ages, they become more forgetful, as a natural process of life. That is understood and cannot be contested. We also know that forgetfulness has degrees of severity and the more severe it gets the more difficult it becomes to treat. We will not get into such detail as the topic can easily glide into the field of medical science where, unfortunately we are not qualified to comment on. The forgetfulness that we seek to deal with here is one, which can be corrected by simply organising and collecting oneself without needing to seek medical attention. However, regardless of the degree of severity of forgetfulness, it is a cause for concern all the same and must be attended to with appropriate remedy.

Forgetfulness has the potential to cost you valuable time and can even cause you to miss some life-changing experiences. What a pity that will be, to miss opportunity because your memory let up at some point. So it is important to acknowledge that accepting any level of forgetfulness no matter how small it may seem, can have grave outcomes at times with such crucial consequences as to determine life or death. A simple thing forgotten could have saved a life and a whole world of time.

Once you begin to notice that forgetfulness is setting in and is beginning to have retrogressive effects on your life and more specifically interfering with your time management efforts, then it's time you took action against. The first action to take after making this realisation is rejecting its hold over your life. Refuse to embrace it by accepting it as your weakness. Doing so attracts more of it to you. Reject it completely.

Begin to make affirmations and declarations about a more positive mind. Seek advice and professional help to improve the capacity of your memory to remember.

Train your mind to develop automatic responses that reject forgetfulness. I am sure you can recall some experiences where forgetfulness cost you dearly, sometimes even to the extent of causing you emotional pain whenever you recall the incident. For that reason I shall limit my examples to 'light' material but which has serious potential to damage reputation and personality which would have taken you time to build. Have you ever resolved on a good day to be good for once and be early for church or school or any other place? After all the commendable effort you still would get to the venue late because you had forgotten where you had placed your car keys and lost a lot of time looking for them?

Or, have you ever been invited to talk at a business forum where you were highly regarded and well respected? In preparation, you do all the necessary work, and a few minutes after leaving home for your presentation, you get a call from your wife that you forgot your laptop? I think this is the kind of forgetfulness that we are talking about and which can be remedied by taking some simple actions, which have also helped me take charge of my time. Dealing with forgetfulness can have amazing results in freeing a good portion of your time into more productive use, than spending hours of searching for misplaced keys, or driving back home in traffic jams to collect a gadget.

1. **Your mind should stay alert and responsive**. – agree with your mind to remind you never to place anything down unless you consciously become aware of where you are placing it. Anything that waits for the approval of the conscious mind to happen is easy to bring to remembrance when required, especially if it is a routine task. Have designated places for keeping things of a routine nature, and discipline yourself to cooperate with those conditions – once you train yourself in that manner; you will be surprised that it becomes impossible to misplace anything and valuable time is saved from going to waste.

2. Learn to retrace your steps – Should you misplace that thing anyway, the fastest way to find it is reversing your steps back to where it started. If you get lost anywhere, the best way to recollect yourself is retracing your steps and starting again from where you began. Unless you are living in a world of magic, nothing can be where it has never been taken to. So it is a waste of valuable time to begin looking where you have not been. Go back the way you came, somewhere on that path, you will be able to find your 'keys.'

3. Avoid overloading your mind with too many pending tasks - My experience on this matter, is that you end up having not achieved even one. Rather, attend to them quickly as they come and move on to the next. It is not time saving to partly process one and move to the next only to process it half way and keep piling pending tasks. This is when you need to apply prioritising and scheduling techniques which we shall deal with later. Your mind will not be efficient enough to prioritise the tasks and present them for processing in order of priority, which would ensure a better coordinated effort resulting in time saving. If you just approach these tasks haphazardly without planning well for them, you will definitely lose time. It is not time wasting, to take time to plan for your time.

It is interesting to note that while the advice given in this section may appear to be too simple, it is well worth noting too, that these seemingly simple ideas make a world of a difference in creating time and value for the seemingly difficult tasks. The difference is significant enough to separate super achievement from mediocrity. Taking these simple steps and committing to their success can be rewarding experience. Personally, I feel I am making better progress since I discovered these simple ideas. What is the use of waking up an hour before others to read, and then spending half of your head-start looking for the book? Get organised, cooperate with your mind and stop being unnecessarily forgetful. Use these tactics in combination and you will be amazed by the results.

Here are your Time Inspired actions for Chapter 3.

1. Identify all the bad 'time values' that sit in your subconscious mind as a result of the programming that you received and write them down.

2. Resolve to take action to break associations with such values as they do not respect or support your desire to be time efficient. The above tactics can be a good starting point.

3. Re-programme your mind with beliefs and values that support your desire to take responsibility of your time.

4. Find an item, symbol, music, phrase or whatever it is and use it as a trigger to keep you alert. Each time you see it, it should remind you to be conscious of the passage of time and the need to take action.

5. Purpose to organise yourself.

Chapter 5

Develop a lifelong 'budget' for your time

"When planning for a year plant corn; when planning for a decade plant trees and when planning for life train and educate society." – Chinese Proverb

What is the plan for your time? What are you planting? Because what you plant tells us a story about the level of commitment you are prepared to invest. Budget your time, for your entire life. They say, *'whatever gets budgeted for, gets done.'*

The Strategy – develop a systematic way of managing time.

If your organisation was under an imminent attack from someone, or another institution, with a well-established reputation for performance and good track record in the area of attack, and the attacking had the potential to destroy you: what would your natural reaction be if your intention was to fight this destruction? I think the first step would be to have an awareness of the imminent threat, and then gather information about its source. When the adversary has been identified then survival options can be explored. Meaning to say different adversaries will require different strategies and an appropriate approach for each. In this case (our case) the adversary is known (time), which makes the planning easier as it can straight away be targeted. In planning for combat where the enemy is known the approach would be to study its system thoroughly and familiarise with its routine. Learn its strengths and weaknesses, and from there develop your own strategy to challenge it.

Once satisfied with the intelligence so gathered, internal capacity is assessed to determine the ability to challenge the opponent.

Where capacity is lacking, external expertise should be engaged to assist with technical support, training, supply of essential equipment, etc. Rigorous training then follows almost assimilating near battle situation. Take note that in the whole process, although experts and supporters are at your disposal, it is you or your institution that has to go through the entire process.

It means you work the hardest of all organs involved, and it is ultimately you that shall face the consequences of the battle. Supporters may offer you help, temporary refuge, hiding space, etc., but you must be the one firmly on the ground and directing operations. This is military style in my view, given my limited knowledge of it which is certainly borrowed from watching war movies on television. I hope I have managed to capture all the important details required on preparing for combat.

This is precisely the intention of the writer of this book, to influence the reader to consider framing a strategy of facing time in their lives. The writer contends that a purposeful life is impossible without a plan for time. If we do not plan for it, our lives will lack direction and will have no 'leadership' to guide the progress we so wish for in life.

The case for an individual

Let me introduce a scenario to test this idea. Imagine you were to wake up tomorrow and be told that you no longer had your job, and was asked to go home. Let's give you time to recover from the shock of the news. Suppose now after the shock, you are back to your senses, and enough time has elapsed for you to have recovered from the effects of the news and have accepted the new reality and you are ready to move on with life. Where do you start? Do you have a personal time schedule to fall back on, with signposts that say by the year 2015, I should have....................., by 2018 my last child must have completed high school, and I should have done etc etc?

What will guide the direction for your next action now that the thing (your work) that dictated your time allocation all along is no more? For most people, work has taken over the responsibility of deciding and determining how they use their time with them having no clue of this arrangement.

Remember earlier we said, time operates within an organised system, and we also said, you cannot have a fighting chance with time, if you don't have an organised system to follow. Because this is the nature of time, it requires that you have one (system) of your own, somehow. Because organisations realise this fact, they organise and plan for their time. They employ you, and you run with their plan for your time. If one does not have this plan in place, certainly something else will take that place and plan on your behalf. Imagine how your work or job determined the time you woke up, the time spent with your family, the time you gave to personal development, etc.

If you had no plan such as the one being suggested above, it means you will not have a personal motivator to influence your decisions concerning your time henceforth. In that situation, nothing objective drives your time allocation and use. All of a sudden, you find yourself with too much time for which you have no clear plan. But remember, the cost of unplanned, unnoticed, unmanaged time! Don't allow your time to glide into these territories. The consequences are too heavy to bear. If, on the other hand, the plan was in place, then after the crying period in the above scenario, you would get up, dust yourself and look at your plan to see how far you have gone into that plan. You can even be guided in reallocating your new-found time to the next pending point on your plan. Your plan will provide the motivation you need to carry on with life. It means you quickly get back to the rhythm of life than waking up and staying in bed with no idea as to what to do next or where to start. Meanwhile, time does not stop. It keeps going while you keep crying.

The foregoing is the reason why we keep insisting that people, as well as organisations should develop strategic plans for their time, which span their entire lives. But how possible is it to come up with a watertight strategy against time? This is certainly a tough call. It is a fact that we can never succeed in 'micro managing' time. However, the fact stands; you can never have a winning battle with time, if you don't have a systematic way of facing it. Have that organised system that you commit to and follow consistently, even if it is not a perfect system. At least, you have a starting point. Do your best to come up with one that best suits your life! And always remember, the bit that your strategy cannot address after your personal effort, will find redress in the Divine, because our human nature makes it impossible to account for every moment that passes in our lives.

However, for now suffices to say, the Divine should be a vital part of your strategy. Whatever strategy you decide to come up with always acknowledge the role of God. He has a big part to play in support of your effort. Those many small moments that slip out of our hands, land in his domain. In chapters that follow, we take time to study how God himself has dealt with time, and it is from there that we adopt the solutions we offer in this book. The last chapter of the book, features the role that God plays in showing His support for man in his quest to conquer time, and shows how it is possible to defy time when God comes to our side.

So now, just to be sure we are on the same page and making sense, let us just give a simple definition of 'strategy' and point out a few important aspects relevant to this discussion. Let us now move away from the military zone and come closer to home, with our borrowed ideas from the war front as this was our case study.

'A strategy is a high level plan to achieve a certain goal(s) under conditions of uncertainty.'

The necessity of a strategy arises out of the need to ensure one's survival in an environment that is unforgiving. It is more like in a do-or-die situation. Every living individual or existing organisation finds themselves in this scenario, by virtue of their existence, when it comes to time. No matter what stage of life or growth they are at in their lives, they still have to contend with time. It's like they both have no choice, but are forced to have one (a strategy). People should realise that not having one is a plan on its own, but which you have no ownership of and therefore, cannot commit to. It is a high level plan as well, but this time to fail. Because there is no method to follow, any road will do, and anyhow. Imagine the massacre to your camp if your opponent had to come with a well organised plan for battle, and all you had was an armed force but without a plan. It's like challenging a video game which you have never played. It will outsmart you, hands down. The same experience is what time will do if you approached it without a plan.

Where a strategy is in place, goals are set, and plans to achieve them, allocating resources to ensure that the goals are realised in the prescribed manner. A strategy can be intended, meaning that there is an intention right from the start to have it, or it may be imposed by the need to adapt to the environment, or else you die a natural death.

The last aspect of strategy that I wish to talk about and, which is important is that a strategy is driven by the top-most person in the organisation or by the leadership. In the case of an individual, it's a case of self-leadership; the individual becomes the CEO of his faculties and hence the driver of the strategy.

That means if your goal was to read a book, for example, you commit to this goal, you coordinate all members of your body concerned in the reading process, ie. the eyes, the mind, the health, etc. to make sure the book is read. If you have to buy spectacles to help aid the reading, then you allocate resources to make sure that the glasses are acquired. You create the conditions that promote the reading of the book. That is strategy implementation at the individual level. You are the driver of the strategy.

Since we are planning to craft a strategy for time, against our lives, and we know that time shall still affect our lives in the future, that means our plan has to be a life time strategy, because for as long as we live, time shall always be our problem to contend with. Make a 'time' budget covering every crucial stage of life. Identify where you are today and start budgeting the time for those stages you haven't reached. Generally, the most crucial stages of life span twenty years each, and so you can already see that there is not enough time in any one of these stages. Break them down further, you discover that you have no time left to spare.

The free dictionary defines the age of a person as: *'The length of time that a person or thing has existed'*. So in essence it defines how far one has gone on the journey of life, and also reveals how much is left in terms of the general direction of life. For instance, if you are 18, then you will know that you are still in the first stage of the 20 year periods. So life progresses in a natural sequence, and we have just summarised it below. There is obviously a lot of detail not included here, but as you set out to make you own plan, you will discover the realities of what you have to deal with in that period of your life.

Child hood – the early stages in the existence of a being.

Youth – time of life between childhood and adulthood.

Adulthood – a period of time in your life after your physical growth has stopped, and you are fully developed. In other words, at this stage you are capable of performing every function expected of a creature of your species. And this naturally becomes the period when pressure for time begins to mount.

Bachelorhood – time of a person's life prior to marriage

Middle age - the period of human life between youth and old age

Old age – a late time of life

Deathbed – last moments before death

These are some of the periods in life that will be crucial in coming up with your time budget.

You can have ten-year plans, for instance, where you define milestones which you must target to have achieved by the end of a period, after which you review and adjust your plan for the future, based on prevailing conditions and progress made.

For example, your milestones for your sixth decade should not have tasks that are labour intensive. Remember as time passes, your resources which enable you to achieve goals are depleting and require continual monitoring to make sure you assign appropriate tasks for achievement of goals, as suggested in earlier notes

You cannot, start having ambitions to become an athlete at the age of 70, for example. So your goal setting has to be realistic in that sense. Be relevant in your planning. Take these as principles to guide your planning process. Think strategically, plan strategically.

The case for business

For organisation, this long-range planning, that we have talked about should also be adopted. In business circles it is commonly referred to as The Strategic Planning of the business.
It is critical that this plan, though long term, be 'punctuated', with shorter term interventions such as periodic reviews of, say, yearly, depending on the industry involved, than is the case with strategy for the individual.

The pace of business evolution, technological advancements, and many other variables in the business environment are so rapid that plans that often go beyond a 5-year period without a dynamic adaptation strategy may become inappropriate and would put the organisation at risk. The end result is a slow and natural death for the organisation.

Naturally, all companies traverse the business landscape in phases or stages, with different approaches adopted for each phase. I like the way James Manktelow puts it in his article, "The Product Life Cycle" on 'The Mind Tools' page. He says, "*Just as people go through infancy, childhood, adulthood and old age, so too do products and brands. And just as we swing from being needy, to being overall contributors to our families or to society, and then back to being needy again over the course of lives, so - in effect - do products*". What determines this progression in any business is the product. The business is inclined to model its operations in line with the direction dictated by the product as it passes through its various stages of growth. Different companies selling different products will experience different periods in these stages as products differ in the way they progress.

The four phases usually used to describe a product's life cycle are – Introduction, Growth, Maturity, and Decline. These stages are best depicted on a commonly referred to model called the Product Life Cycle with each stage being expressed as a function of time and coming one after another as shown in the diagram in fig 2.

Product Life cycle

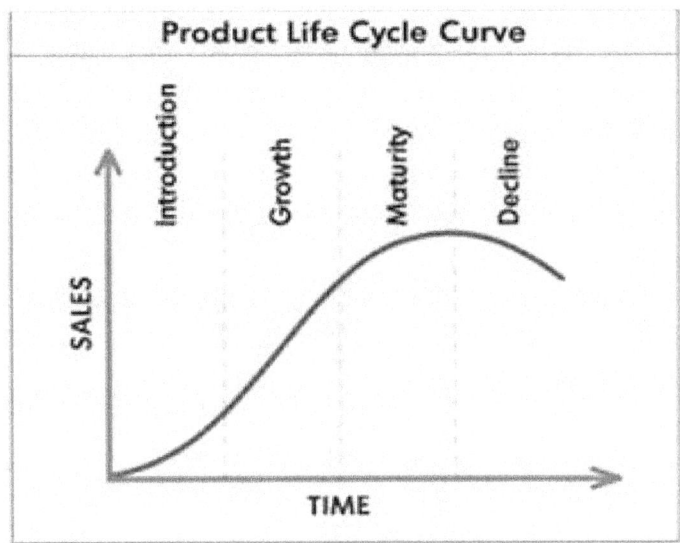

Figure 2

Used in combination with the strategic objectives of an organisation, and other initiatives this model can provide useful information in recommending appropriate marketing tactics to employ for any of the stages it suggests.

The big idea in applying this model is the change that occurs to marketing initiatives adopted by the company in the various stages as they come. Understanding this model and the demands that come with each stage of the product life, will not only be useful to the marketers, but can also be a valuable tool for 'time planners' or top management of the company as they plan resources for each stage.

It provides management with information required to determine nature of activities that can be approved to happen during each phase, and those that can be shelved or dropped, in response to time demands of that particular stage on the available human resources. During the introduction stage, for example, the demand for the marketing effort will be high and management will be inclined to take decisions that support this direction.

Among other considerations, an assessment of the requirement needs of the stage can reveal the demand for managerial time required to effectively carry out the dominant tasks of that stage, such as heavy promotional work, heavy advertising activities, etc. Just by knowing what to expect in each stage, management can then make relevant interventions to smoothen the work load and allocate time optimally. In this case, they may, for example, decide to:

1. Release the already overstrained managerial capacity in terms of 'time load', by approving the outsourcing of all promotional material for that particular time.

2. Recruit an experienced marketer, specifically to handle this promotional activity.

This releases managerial time for other pressing commitments, which might not have received their deserved attention such as, say, obtaining health certification for the products the company is promoting, and presents the manager with better chance to achieve success. So this kind of resource evaluation should be carried out for each stage of the product life cycle and priority given to critical life defining tasks for the company for that particular phase.

In chapters that follow, we shall revisit the concept of time being a finite resource in greater detail. It is this concept which we have exploited here to come up with the ideas we have suggested in this section. I will just pre-empt and briefly explain the concept. It considers or recognises time as a resource that is limited in supply, just like any other resource owned by the company and as such should only be allocated to activities which it can optimally 'finance'. What this basically means is that the company has to assess feasibility of delivery of a good result by a manager before assigning a new or additional task.

What amount of time is demanded by this new activity? Does the person intended for the task have the capacity to absorb it in the available time without compromising quality of work? If they cannot objectively justify or verify these facts, then they seriously have to consider making adjustments to the activity to a level where it can become feasible.

Assuming that this company was established to produce only one product, and that no other interventions will be carried out at any stage of the life of the product, then it is easy to determine that the life of that company depends entirely on the life cycle of its product. So the entire life of an organisation can be predicted purely on this basis, and management can now be guided by applying timely interventions at the relevant stages of the product life cycle to perpetuate the life of their organisation. So engaging into any kind of business without regard to the knowledge of the phase or stage in which your product(s) is in, may really affect your chances of survival. At best, you could copy initiatives being employed by your competition, but their advantage over you is that theirs is a well-planned action that considers a number of factors, including the most crucial resource - time. In the table below we try to summaries all these ideas and come up with guidelines for a life-long strategy for both individuals and companies.

Guide lines for a Strategic Plan for managing time

Time Strategy	Individual	Organisation
Develop life Long Goals Be a visionary	Have a vision, of where you are going. You can only truly celebrate the achievement of a fulfilled and purposeful life when you reach your final goal(s).	The Vision provides direction and focus. We can forecast way into the future of our business, living in the dream of the visionary leaders of the company.
Have Short Term Goals and define your Milestones.	Break it down into manageable tasks to avoid being intimidated by sight of huge and seemingly undoable tasks. For achievement of current and short term desire.	Divide the big chunk into manageable and doable tasks to encourage progress. To meet operational plans whose direction is guided by the vision, tackling set milestones along the way as you go.
Method	• Continuous training of oneself to manage time • Conditioning of the mind to cooperate with expressed desire to manage time well. • Developing mechanisms & tactics that continue to support the desire to manage time. • Goal setting that reflects time sensitivity. Have systems to assist your effort to schedule your time such as programs, time schedules, diaries planners etc. • Set Your Milestones, suited to your conditions, that you focus all your energies to accomplish, & which guide you to the bigger picture. • Balance your time planning considering the importance, priority and relevance of all purposeful activities of life. • Build a legacy that launches your influence well into the future after you are gone	• Developing an organisational culture that is time sensitive. • Conducting Time Training for all employees. • Develop a 'Time Policy' & Implement it company-wide. • Establish & follow your Time management framework for guidance –Time Scheduling, Master calendars, programs, etc. • Invest in technologies that improve Time efficiency at all critical stages of the business especially at management level. • Use your Strategic Plan as the compass as you pass through your set Milestones. • As demand for your limited time keeps growing, balance becomes key. Allocate requisite time to all your managerial tasks.
Focus	• Ranking & prioritising life tasks and allocating time	• Efficient use of the time resource in line with broad

	slots according to their weight in line with the aspirations and life goals. • Ensuring balance by making sure that all aspects of life are allocated time in proportion to their weight.	objectives of the Co. • Minimise on waste of time and ultimately money. • Mechanisms to monitor usage and security of time
Resources	• Time • Your mind, • Your Energy/power. • people • appropriate materials that support the effort- books, videos, documentaries etc	• Corporate Time, • money, • people, employees, Managers • technology • organisational energy
Ultimate goal	Fulfilled life on earth and preparation for the afterlife	Profitable Organisation that transcends the life of its promoters.
Driver of strategy	Oneself	Management
Success factors	• Prayer & acknowledgement of the role of The Almighty in managing time • Self-Mastery • Consistency in implementing • Carefully selected Supporters • Trained/conditioned Mind • Supportive structures – accountability partners etc • Celebrate successes daily • Take your chances when they come. • Develop your faith in God • Never ignore ethical & moral considerations • Speed	• Technology, information • Role of Facilitator/Change agent – results oriented • Visionary Leadership & commitment • Cultured people • Buy in from employees • Celebrate successes • Performance appraisal targeted at time usage • System that Identify time leakages and plugs them. • Take your chances • Never ignore ethical considerations • speed
Motivation	Desire to be in control of my 'now' and avoid blame from 'future' me.	Organisational Culture - values, norms, symbols etc

Cont…..

Process	Strategic thinking – process should align with ultimate achievement of one's purpose.	Strategic planning – the process should make reference to the strategic objectives of the organisation, and lead to attainment of the vision.
Prerequisites	Knowing Your purpose	Clear Vision
Threats	Treating time as an infinite resource Procrastination Lack of Money, Dwindling Energy, Lack Self- belief, Untrained mind Unmanaged time Failure to assert your own time values Failure to balance time allocation Eternal potential Failure to deal with slowness	Treating time as an infinite resource Procrastination Mismatch of time allocations with strategic priorities, Lagging behind in technology, people, uncultured leadership, no or poor corporate culture unplanned change unmanaged time lack of balance

Table 4

I cannot over emphasize the importance of taking this step in one's life. You simply need to develop an organised system to manage your time, and that's why we give some guidelines above. It's even more critical in organisations because of the need to coordinate events, departments, individuals, subsidiaries, etc. In that previous job I referred to earlier, we used to have meetings that would stretch for hours, at the expense of production. The whole department would sit in that meeting, and each person would wait for their turn to report on their territory. Those coming from outside towns would be given priority to enable safe travel back to their towns.

There is one particular meeting, that everyone in the department dreaded, and it happened to be a monthly meeting. It would start after lunch and proceed into the evening. On that day, even customers had to wait. Once time planning became a priority for the organisation, after realising its value, all that became a thing of the past. The meeting dates would now be set by dedicated staff, booked on the master calendar, and we became equipped each with planners and diaries. On the date of the meeting, each was given a time slot to attend and report. You now knew that I can be productive all day and only arrive on time for my appointment and get back to work when done. This new effort and more of course had tremendous results for the company. Not only in having an efficient time management system, but also contributed to the bottom line. More time was released for productive work. So take note; it is never, ever a waste of time, to sit down and plan for your time. Any kind of deliberate planning is by far better than living without one. If you don't plan for time, you live like someone who is in denial, because whatever work that you had to do you still have to do it, but chances are obviously it will be done under pressure, because your time is not evenly distributed.

The plans that we are advocating for here are life time plans for your time. You should be able to tell, if asked, what you will be doing 20 years from now according to your planning. Of course, the details will come as you approach the milestone, but the broad direction should guide how you direct your time now.

Here are some actions you can begin to take to start taking charge of your time

Crucial factors to consider before your 'time budget'

Action	Individual	Organisation
Reflect on progress to date	• How far have you gone into life? • Do you or have you ever considered managing your time with a broad perspective spanning your entire lifetime? • Are you living a purposeful life? • Do you have a personal connection with the divine?	• How far have you gone into your product lifecycle? • Have you made long range plans for your company guided by stages of your product life cycle? • Is the direction of your company determined by your long range plans or vision?
Reflect on your purpose	• Have you discovered your purpose yet? • If yes, evaluate progress and refocus • If no, consider knowing your purpose today. It's not possible to convince yourself to tie yourself to a long term time plan, if this is not clear.	• Are you clear about the strategic direction of your organisation? • If yes evaluate progress and adapt to prevailing conditions? • If no, it's imperative that you have sight of the plan and align all your efforts to it taking into consideration current stage of business.

Cont……

Using the guidelines above to create a long range program for managing your time	• Which of the periods highlighted above do you belong? Your plan should take this into consideration • Develop a lifetime plan with milestones along the way. • Seek personal contact with God	Consider how far your organisation has travelled along its life cycle. And guide your time management with requisite demand for your current stage. Plan for stages ahead and have time budgets for them.

Table 5

Chapter 6
Even Business should develop a time-conscious culture

In as much as time is proving to be a scarce resource for any purposeful individual's life, so it is also in the life of organisations or institutions. Time remains scarce. More-so because no rational organisation can exist without a clear purpose. Once purpose comes into the picture, there is never enough time to allocate to all the necessities required to fulfilling that purpose. So the same way a purposeful individual is pressed for time during his lifetime, it is the very same way a visionary organisation is also pressed. In my previous job, I worked in a position that would generally be equated to the job of a Sales Executive; time was just not enough in that job, no matter how many hours you tried to put into it, or was it simply poor planning? I barely had time for anything else. You had to follow strict deadlines; targets for reporting; a rigid master calendar; scheduled meetings; routine meetings; scheduled training for the job, and also those training sessions conducted by me.

Above all that, I had daily tasks, which included mandatory visits to customer sites, which basically generated input for all these scheduled events. As if that was not enough, the company continuously launched new products in the market, and some of them brought along change associated with their implementation, and this further put strain on already over stretched time. Could I cope? I must admit; it was a tough call. I struggled to be on top of the game. It was overwhelming. In case you are beginning to think that maybe I was the one with the problem. If you would to come to the marketing office, around 10 pm, of any day of the week, it was not uncommon to be greeted by the full marketing team busy at it, each on his desk doing his job. At one time, I went on a working visit, to a subsidiary in another country; I was
The magic was in how they managed astonished to find that people in the same job category as mine, were even referred to as magicians.

to survive such pressures and complete tasks within the limited time resource.

So maybe it was the marketing team that was disorganised, was it? The whole marketing team, would retire for the day and go home quite late, but would leave the finance people still at it. I don't know what time they would eventually leave for their homes. This did not seem to me to be just a seasonal load of work, which would subside at some point, because for as long as I remember the finance team seemed genuinely busy and had loads and loads of work. Were they also disorganised? My entry point in that company before I moved to marketing was the Operations department. During my first days at the place, everyone had a question for me. *"Are you married yet young man? Because if you come to this company before you do, chances are you will never marry"* they would say. There simply was no time for anything else besides work. The company even introduced shifts, to try to cope with demand for production that meant that my daytime was taken, the evenings were taken; the weekends and holidays were taken, and so I began to see reality in their fears for me.

These shifts were certainly the last nail on the coffin because my only few free hours were now taken by this new arrangement. The only few hours I would be away from work were at odds with time for social events – family, friends etc. My entire social life was rendered dead. Anyway, against all the odds, I got married during the time I was working in that department. I mention this particular detail for two reasons, firstly, to unbundle a puzzle that I gave somewhere at the beginning of the book. I am sure you remember, and you must have the answer by now. I did say that you would figure out as we went deeper into the book. Hope you have by now. And secondly, to support the idea of maintaining balance in the way one allocates time to important tasks in life. For me, marriage was a milestone which I had to have accomplished by a certain time of my life, and against all odds, I did.

Anyway, If you have had a chance to work for a big organisation before, the picture which I have tried to paint above should not be news to you. It seems to happen to almost every company now. So, what's wrong with companies? Or is it the people that are employed there who can't plan their time well? I will leave that question for you to answer.

This scenario has become a growing trend world-wide. The constraints or pressures on this resource have become as pronounced in business as companies battle to stay afloat. Expert researchers have revealed findings proving how bad time management is affecting the 'bottom line'- profitability, and the potential savings that could be achieved just by becoming more time efficient in business. They implore on companies to treat time as a resource that is finite. It should be treated like any other resource owned by a company, realizing and accepting that it also gets depleted and should be safeguarded.

As McKinsey & Company put it, in their article - *Making time management the organisation's priority* "*The impact of always on communications, the growing complexity of global organisation, and the pressures imposed by profound economic uncertainty have all added to a feeling among executives that there are simply not enough hours in the day to get things done.*

As alluded to earlier, you can never stand a chance with time, if you do not have your own organised system to manage it. According to the article by McKinsey, they say…

"*Our research and experience suggest that Leaders who are serious about addressing this challenge must stop thinking about time management as primarily an individual problem and start addressing it institutionally. Time management isn't just a personal-productivity issue over which companies have no control; it has increasingly become an organisational issue whose root causes are deeply embedded in corporate structures and cultures. Fortunately, this also means that the problem can be tackled systematically.*"

The challenges we have seen above and more make it imperative that time management became an organisational issue which is dealt with at the policy-making level of a business. That is to suggest innovation where a company comes up with what I want to call a Time Policy. The single most important aim of this policy would be to drive strategic objectives of the organisation by providing resources and support structures that ensure balance and proportionate allocation of time to tasks in order of their importance to achieve intended results efficiently. Researches carried out across the globe on how managers allocate time to activities they perform daily, show that on average about 50% of managers do not concentrate sufficiently on guiding the strategic direction of the business. In other words, what this means was that managers' 'time use' patterns are not in full alignment with the company's big dreams.

Right there, we can begin to appreciate that time management challenges, and paying little attention to them, do have an influence on the well-being of companies worldwide. Because if half the managers in the world across all sectors of business are engaged full time, but in activities which either delay or counter or do not directly propagate the intended motives of the businesses they manage, then it is a sign of the depth and how widespread the problem is. Time is simply not being efficiently used. I cannot, however, vouch 100% for the above statistic but, still insist that it gives signal enough to provoke thought among the company leaders, and persuade them to take stock of the level of guidance they give to their managers insofar as the way they use their time to promote the vision of the company. So this new 'Policy' should be seen to create conditions that ensure the execution and attainment of the broad objectives of the organisation in the most efficient manner.

If you envisage a company whose corporate structures reflect this kind of thinking, it should not be a misnomer to find along-side that company's vision and mission statements; a statement of how they use their time- a Time Policy if I may call it. The statement should show the significance, the values espoused, and the culture followed by the organisation pertaining to their use of the time resource. This statement would also be framed and posted in strategic locations within the organisation, and most importantly positioning it where 'outsiders' and visitors to the company are greeted with that same message. That is particularly important in that it demonstrates an intention and priorities. I have not seen this yet in any organisation, but of course, that does not eliminate the possibility that other companies have already discovered its value. The question is, how much attention are you giving to this resource as a manager in your own organisation?

Peter Drucker in his famous dictum about time says: *"Time is the scarcest resource, and unless it is managed nothing else can be managed."*

The moment this idea is adopted, it means the company, rather than individuals take over the responsibility of managing this very precious resource. The company can now come up with systematic methods of dealing with the time problem, and can even provide institutional support, resources, incentives and tools necessary to make it effective. Senior managers can create time budgets and formal processes for allotting time.

In the organisation that I worked for, whenever an issue found itself in the arena of policy formulation, the management would engage experts to develop the idea. Once they were satisfied with the final product from the consulting firms, they would come up with innovative ways to disseminate the information to every employee. In one such occasion, they made parcels for every employee which was packaged in very attractive bags, to reflect the level of importance I guess.

The small bags carried a lot of accessories, which depicted in various ways the message they intended to deliver. These included among other things, posters, stickers, pens, symbols, ceremonial objects, etc. In addition to all those things, was a letter signed by the chairman of the company with the message engraved onto it. To reflect the importance of this message, the chairman of the region would then schedule trips to visit every affiliate under him to personally deliver and follow up on the message by word of mouth. You were sure that after such visit, a series of sessions on the subject would follow. And guess what, the issue would find its way into the performance appraisal process. It was a means to ensure and enforce these strategic values among staff, and I can assure you it worked, although as employees, we never really appreciated the value of that effort.

I remember at that time, being employees, as usual; we would scoff at such initiatives. We would try to calculate the value of the packaged goods, the airfares involved in the chairman's travels, the hotel bills, the training sessions held etc. and converted that to monetary value. Then after coming up with a figure, we would now try to see what impact all that 'wasted' money would have had on our pockets had they given us a raise instead. I think of it now and I appreciate that effort now that I run my own business. They were simply pushing strategic interests. This to me was a demonstration of a leadership that was determined to guide the strategic direction of their organisation. It comes as no surprise that the very message that was packaged in those bags, now works in my own business, and I find use of its application even in this book. At a later stage, we shall talk about ethical considerations in time management, and it is there that I shall share with you, two of the virtues that we were taught, namely; cross functionality, and mutual support. It makes sense to me now how these two qualities join in to improve time management of an organisation. Below I shall suggest a few tactics or approaches that senior managers can employ to effectively influence the direction of the company by managing time.

Acknowledge the value of Corporate Time

As a first step towards transforming your organisation's time culture, effort has to be exerted for employees to begin to develop an appreciation of the value of corporate time to your organisation. Realise that corporate time is already paid for in general. That's why even if I come to sleep at work, and you have no means of monitoring and controlling that, you are still obliged to pay me. The moment you employ someone; you have, in essence, bought their freedom of time use, and it automatically becomes the organisation's time. Once it becomes that, it becomes part of the business's property the same way you would pay for an asset and claim possession of it. As a general rule, an employer must therefore compensate their employees for the time that they have surrendered under their control and being of benefit to them.

Do you realise that the moment that time passes the boundary from 'personal time' to corporate time; nothing changes in the values held by that person, unless the company employs measures to do so? The 'time' values held by that individual have simply been transferred to the employer. If the employer does not take steps to upgrade this value, it means the company will be limited only to the values held by that individual for application in their company. And that's how many companies are operating today, and boy! does it smack of trouble! Would a business entity be satisfied with this kind of arrangement? If it had to employ 100 people and not do anything else to add value to their time beliefs, it means the company will have 100 sets of time belief systems. This factor alone gives merit to the idea propounded by McKinsey above. Organisations should find ways to make their employees adapt to their culture, if they have any.

Take for example, would you act the same way at a football match as a spectator, as you would while watching a documentary at a business forum? If in either situation, you behaved as you would have in the other situation, the other participants in either scenario, would make it clear, in no uncertain terms, that your behaviour was not in conformity to what they considered appropriate. The time values held by the employee have to be guided by the values espoused by the organisation. If this is not important, why do you send employees, especially new ones for induction training? Why should time lessons be the only part of the individual which the company cares little to change? Maybe it's an oversight, but I would want to think that in most instances, companies have no idea as to what to teach about time. This leads to the next point.

Develop your organisational Time Culture
Right from the start, school your employees on the time values you embrace as an organisation. If this curriculum is not there, it's time to go back to the Strategic Document driving the direction of the company and start crafting a 'Time Culture' for your organisation, that aligns and influences employee behaviour in a manner that is desirable to the organisation. Every company has its own unique personality, just like people do. The unique personality of an organisation is referred to as its culture. Organisational culture is a system of shared values, assumptions, and beliefs, which govern how people behave in the organisation. These shared values have a strong influence on the people in the organisation and dictate how they behave, dress, and perform in their jobs. A strong organisational culture is the easiest way you can identify deviant behaviour among employees and quickly rectify the same before bad habits develop and spread. It's not just enough to have it, school them and enforce it.

Have a system to monitor, support and evaluate time values of the organization

As management, you should reflect your priorities in the way you assign tasks to your subordinates. The duties you assign to your juniors should have SMART objectives always. This leaves you in a good position to monitor progress, support where signs indicate a need, and assess efficiency. If your duties lack any of these guiding principles, you may have trouble to objectively evaluate the performances. The objectives you set should be:

Specific – targeting a specific area of improvement which you deliberately selected.

Measurable –they should be quantifiable, or at least suggest an indicator of progress.

Assignable – should specify who will do it,

Realistic - State what results can realistically be achieved, given the available resources.

Time-related – specify when the results should be achieved. You can break it into manageable tasks to achieve the big dream and each being guided by time.

The sum total of these small attributes is what will help you evaluate performance during an appraisal of the employee at the end of an agreed period.

Provide quality administrative support

The fact that we highlighted the need for the company to, upon employing an individual, train them, monitor their performance and evaluate their contribution, etc, naturally imposes a responsibility on the companies to offer support to their employees in their quest to managing their time efficiently and in line with the organisation's objectives. Resources that can be offered by companies on this front include, highly qualified and motivated administrative personnel such as a Personal Assistant to each key manager, for example.

These are highly trained persons, with demonstrable records of success in driving and managing the time aspect of high ranking managers in the organisation. If the correct persons occupy this position, it could very well make the difference between an efficiently run organisation and one that is poorly managed.

Invest in technology that responds to your needs
A company that invests in technology that assists in meeting its strategic objectives demonstrates their depth of intention. When employees see equipment or machinery bought for a particular stated purpose, they read into the seriousness of intent, and naturally are obliged to take the initiative seriously. In my previous job, when the company started sending all company vehicles for installation of tracking devices; we got the picture. The guys were serious. The devices provided among other things, information useful for diary analysis. This would be studied to see if your movements matched with company objectives and whether corporate time was being used productively.

Of course being an employee that sounded barbaric, especially if you had worked before in an environment without such restrictions, but I can testify to the effectiveness of implementing such a system in terms of enforcing discipline on time usage and aligning it to company objectives. The resistance offered by employees only shows the lack of 'buy-in' from employees as a result of poor communication by management, of the intention and the anticipated benefits from adopting the system. If they had a kind of committee that championed change and had disseminated the information well, the reception would have been better, and the initiative would have yielded results much earlier. If I was to advise them, I would advocate for some kind 'formal' committee to handle such tasks, and this forms my next discussion point.

Other forms of technology worth considering, includes computer-based software that assists in analysing how time usage by managers met their individual strategic objectives.

All these and more are initiatives that help to reset internal governance structures within organisations, and the savings from such initiatives are so huge you could even start another company. According to self-praise statements given by the suppliers of such software, they say 2000 to 5000 person- hours of executive time stand to be recovered annually and at the same time improving drastically on strategic focus. Now tell me if this is not a worthwhile venture, even if on actual implementation, you are only able to recover half of their claimed benefit. It's a lot of money if you ask me and with the elusiveness of the dollar in our time, the consultant that prescribes such a remedy truly deserves a big reward.

Establish a formal Governance Committee
To complement the above objective it is necessary to form a team that champions the cause. An organisation can have formal time systems and establish a committee tasked with the responsibility of creating, managing, preserving and perpetuating the time culture of an organisation. For this committee to be effective, it must command the respect of employees, and the composition of the committee should include a member of the management committee, or a member of top management heading the committee. The selected member must among other qualities be a highly motivated time-conscious individual and who has a good manager-employee relationship. The role or domain of this committee is overseeing time budgets for company-wide initiatives.

The committee has the mandate to oversee the time budgetary process and give its approvals of the same, once it is satisfied. It monitor the company's "time health status" through the various resources availed to it by the company, and chart a way forward for the organisation in-as-far as time management issues are concerned. Among its responsibilities should be the task of assessing managerial capacity, in terms of time to handle demands of intended projects. The committee makes recommendations that would move the business in the best possible direction as it efficiently allocates time. All change of significance should first also be evaluated by this committee and approved by it.

Have time budgets for Leadership in priority initiatives.

"Establishing a time budget for priority initiatives might sound radical, but it's the best way to move toward the goal of treating leadership capacity as companies treat financial capital and to stop financing new initiatives when the human capital runs out." McKinsey & Company in their article quoted above.

If the above suggestion is followed satisfactorily even at managerial level, it aligns or matches the organisation's capacity to handle new or additional assignments to any manager. The scenario is analogous to a situation where an organisation identifies a lucrative opportunity and expresses the desire to adopt it. Before they can resolve to take on the project, they assess their financial capability to determine whether they have a good financial ground to see through the implementation of the project. If the financial resources are not adequate to perform the task, the organisation is more likely to let it pass or shelve it until such a time when resources become available. Alternatively, they would have to scale down on the level of the project to suit the size of the financial resource available.

This adjustment happens because money is regarded and accepted as a limited resource. Now take, for instance, the same scenario happens and the company has all the good reasons to take on the project, and the finances are available. The most obvious and common reaction by management in this case would be to give a thumbs-up to the project to go ahead.

However, what they forget or turn a blind eye on is doing the time audit or diary analysis, to help ascertain feasibility of the company's ability to handle the new task. Time, is a resource the same way money or finances are. If the managers could decide to stop project implementation on account of scarcity of funds, if they are serious and really believe that time is not only a resource, but a finite resource just like any other, including money, then surely they should also evaluate capacity of managers in terms of time competence before they can approve the commencement of the project.

In other words, how much leadership capacity does the company have to 'finance' this great new idea? If the result of their assessment indicates surplus time capacity, then I would say, due diligence has been done, and the project can move to be started and stands a good chance of excellent and efficient implementation. As said earlier, one stands a better chance to battle time if they develop a system of confronting it. It is the purpose of this book to develop a strategy that works. We also agreed that for one to come up with a good strategy, they have to have thorough knowledge of their targeted opponent.

They should devote their time to learning about the opponent's strengths, weaknesses, etc. if they are serious about winning and then from there, develop a strategy that would allow them to succeed. For that reason, from this section going forward, we now shift attention to studying time and its character. As we go, you shall discover as from where some of the advice we have given so far was coming from. So get ready to learn from the creator of time. We start by establishing the foundation upon which all this work is based. It is interesting to note that there seems to be no other laudable attempt to explain time than God, and that's where we begin our journey.

Chapter 7
It's Foundation in God

I propose, at this juncture that 'time' is a mystery. It is a puzzle of many pieces, awaiting mastery. That is what we intend to do in this book. We should at least crack it, and lay a foundation for others to break it open. Humanity has struggled with this entity, for as long as they have known it. Even just understanding it has proven to be a big challenge: we cannot even talk about trying to keep pace with it. It defeats us all systems out when it comes to that. It has eluded our thoughts, our meditation, and our imaginations and still remains unsolved over centuries.

To this day, even great scientists, argue about the state of its existence. Some say that: it is 'absolute', suggesting that it always exists, in the universe, and its existence is independent of any activity, and people live in it, as if enveloped by it. Others say, it is relative, suggesting that, it is merely a numerical order of change that takes place in space. And that we only live in space and not in time. How about that for confusion? In some later sections of the book, as alluded to earlier, we shall visit the spirited attempts by giant minds on the subject. The majority of these great minds and influential lads, ended up by making statements that we can deduce and interpret as having conceded defeat. You will surely be surprised by some of their conclusions.

I find time to be somehow 'special', at least in two unique ways. Firstly, that, there can never be a valid 'time model' outside of God - The Creator, or at least one that makes the assumption of His existence in trying to explain it. Mark R Rushdoony, in his work, *The theology of time*, says, *"Defining time is a problem for autonomous man."* and oh! How so true! Trying to define 'time' without God, will lead to theories that are untrue and difficult to defend and sustain.

The second reason, that makes the subject special, is that it has tended to attract even the cleverest of all people, the world has had to offer, and yet; it has still, managed to elude the intellect of humanity to this day. I don't know who you consider to be the most intelligent person or persons to have walked on the face of the earth. Whoever it is, it always baffles me that all such persons if you care to investigate have, in one way or the other, had an attempt at explaining 'time', and some have even produced documented work on the subject, in whatever area of their best competence.

If men of such extraordinary gifting, having employed their God-given faculties; all, to one thing for so many years and still fail to convince the world about that thing, surely there can be no better evidence of the elusive nature of this thing. It has certainly challenged the intellect of mankind. Some scientists have even gone to the extent of defining 'time' as God. How true is this statement? Is answering this question valuable to our discussion? Well, I would like to validate the answering of the question, by asserting its significance.   Answering it, lays an important foundation for our case in this book. The basis upon which this entire book is written, flows from the answer to the question; "Can time to be equated to God"? So dear reader, let us now begin our jour

GOD AND TIME

Is it true that time is God, or that God is time? What is the True relationship between God and time?

People have come up with many ideas, about 'time' and God. Amongst such, is one, where 'time' has been defined as, or equated to God! It is quite crucial for us to respond or answer to those assertions, because, with our little knowledge about the subject; it is very easy to be swayed and led to the wrong beliefs. This idea (time being God), thrives on a flimsy basis, which rides on ill-informed facts, that God and 'time' share the 'same' qualities, and hence believes, that, this qualifies them to amount to the same thing.

An example of this, is, 'God is invisible, and so is time; God is everywhere, and so is time; God never sleeps, and nor does time; and it goes on and on. While it is true, that some of the attributes seem to agree with the observations which lead to the growth of this doctrine, it goes without saying; that the founders of this thought have very limited understanding of God.

In-fact, I believe, that, the attributes that we ascribe to God are only those which we can perceive and imagine in our minds. Time can never compare to this 'unresolved' being. The same way human beings share in some of His attributes is the same way 'time' shares some of its own with God. How could it have been otherwise?

The source of time is God, and in each of his creation, he gave according to his knowledge, a portion of his own being as evidence of his mastery. Otherwise, how were you ever going to trace it back to Him? If not even a bit, of what is in Him could not be found in His creation, and especially creation such as 'time' which we have no evidence of its creation, apart from our faith. He chose the attributes he willed, to give to each creation, in line with its purpose. Imagine if time could be touched? The chaos in the world would be unbearable. Imagine how many people would attempt to draw it back, by any means possible.

So, God did not have such a plan, that would allow man to manipulate 'time', and so made it the way He did. In my view, this theory is flawed, and does two things. One, that it wrongly elevates 'Time' to the status of God, and two, that it belittles the stature of the Almighty God to the size of His own creation. A lot of other theories around 'time' and God have been developed. We shall briefly touch on them to create a platform of proving that God is more than 'time'. That is the belief we hold in this book and the rest of what remains is an effort to magnify that position. Below are some that we shall tackle.

Some have attempted to prove that **God is NOT God, but He is time.** They argue that 'time' is the 'substance' which brings into reality the manifestation of God's power, and hence it is God. Like we say the Holy Spirit is God because through Him, God performs His works. By the same reasoning, they qualify time to be God. Still more, some have even gone further to declare that 'Time does not need God; it is God who needs time'. Meaning that, God cannot operate without 'time', but time can still perform its duties even without God.

I don't know to what extent you agree with all this, but in a while I shall challenge these views to establish the true relationship. However, before we start that; to allow ourselves time to ponder over these thoughts, let us for a short while explore how this phenomenon called 'time' came into existence. Our contentions here, lay an important foundation in understanding the true relationship between God and time, as well as reveal mysteries surrounding the question of 'time'. So let us now dig into it. Where did time come from?

Chapter 8
Could Time have existed before the beginning?

Let's begin, by making an assertion here, that, 'God is the creator of 'time'. Just as we know, He is the creator of all things.

John 1; 3 all things were made by Him; and without him was not anything made that was made.

Further, regardless of the state of existence of anything, whether it be physical or spiritual, visible or invisible, directly spoken into being or being by the inference of the Almighty, one thing is undeniable; God is the Originator of them all, as long as they exist in the universe. Only those 'things' that exist outside this realm, (the universe), escaped creation.

Colossians 1; 16 For by him, were all things created, that are in heaven, and that are in earth, visible and invisible, whether they be thrones, or dominions, or principalities, or powers: all things were created by him and for him:

This scripture above, has made it clearer, by bringing to the fore, categories of creation, one of which, 'time', can be assigned to. However, if anything by some 'chance', escaped the hand of God in creation, and that thing (obviously should have) existed outside of heaven and earth, (that means; it should have existed before creation of heaven and earth) then, we can deduce, what that thing was. It was an unfathomable atmosphere of chaos, nothingness, monotony and great darkness. This description of an atmosphere of out-and-out disorder, on its own, is inconsistent with the very nature of time. The same way you can attest to the impracticality of light sharing the same space as darkness. When time appears, order and change are established in the atmosphere. So, this precludes the existence of time in that kind of environment, and we know that, this ambience endured until the beginning.

And we know that **Genesis1; 1-2** says: **In the beginning God created the heaven and the earth. And the earth was without form, and void; and darkness was upon the face of the deep. And the Spirit of God moved upon the face of the waters.**

So now, we have managed to eliminate the possibility of time existing before the beginning. Let us simplify it further and just say, 'nothing,' existed before creation, apart from the spirit of God. Anything; therefore, that came after creation, including 'time' became a creation of God. And from the instant of its creation, the operation of 'time' commenced, and the moment later, introduced a change to the universe. Theologian JI Parker puts it aptly, in one of his works; "What is God's relationship to time?"

He says, *"To put it simply, time is duration. Our clocks mark change or, more precisely; our timepieces are benchmarks of change that indicate the passage of time. We could say, then, that time is a necessary precondition for change, and change is a sufficient condition to establish the passage of time. In other words, whenever there is a change of any kind, we know that time has passed. Additionally, the science of physics tells us that time is a property resulting from the existence of matter. As such, time exists whenever matter exists. However, God is not matter; God, in fact, created matter. The bottom line is this: time began when God created the universe. Before that, God was simply existing. Since there was no matter, and because God does not change, time had no existence and therefore, no meaning, no relation to him."*

The theologian paints a vivid picture, of the status quo during the era before 'time'. If we agree, to the notion that *"time is a necessary precondition for change, and that change is a sufficient condition to establish the passage of time"* we can argue therefore, that the inhabitants of the darkness filled existence before the beginning must have never changed.

But evidence of matter- the heavens, the earth, the waters, etc mentioned in the first two verses of the bible suggest that the cause of them all must have been in some kind of motion in order to be able to cause them. Events recorded a few moments after creation of heaven and earth further give weight to this. The later part of verse 2 of Genesis 1 reveals that The Spirit of God was in a state of motion as He hovered over the face of the waters, further confirming His infinitude. Meaning that, before time, God was in motion, and after its creation continued to move, which is not possible if time is not present. He was not bound by it. He had no need of time to be able to operate. It was in-fact, 'time,' that needed God, in order to exist. He has no beginning, because He caused the beginning, and also follows that He has no ending. In other words, He is eternal. So there can never be an argument again, about God being in need of time in order to operate. God is sovereign. He does not depend on anything to perform any task. If He does, He only does it for us, to comprehend.

And so we conclude, in answer to the question that gave birth to this chapter. Though we never hear of the spoken word by God, commanding time to appear, the arguments brought forth in this chapter make it clear that time could not have existed before the creation. It only started in the beginning, at the instruction of God. The next two chapters will validate that position.

Chapter 9
But, is 'the beginning' real?

Maybe if you are like me, at some point in the past; I had no real belief of the beginning. I would just accept it, but with no genuine conviction about it. You are also probably in doubt about the reality of this event. Does the universe really have a beginning? Or is it just an imagined belief? Maybe you share the view that the universe has always existed; and that there can be no point in time, where it can be said to have begun. Is it not just a convenient and clever invention by the proponents of the story of God and His works of creation? Is it not just a suitable reason to justifying the bible, but without real proof to substantiate the claim, except for what is written in the bible? But why labour so much on this point, (the beginning), when our real issue, in essence, is to prove 'time'?

If it was me, to answer that question, my response would be, 'The more reason to'. If it's true that time exists, and we agree that it measures duration or is a benchmark of change, then from good sense, a beginning is important, and inevitable. So, proving that indeed 'there was a beginning' is so significant a step and necessary to validate the existence of 'time'. My conviction, now, is that, indeed, there was a beginning, which became the starting point, of not only 'time', but also, all other things. Time had the singular honour and privilege to signal the beginning, by ticking from that moment called the beginning. It is the absolute reference point to which we can trace back the passage of time.

So then, prove the beginning!

So let us journey back to that moment, to see if we can prove it. Well, for a start, I don't know, and I can't comprehend why, for some reason, anyone would want to convince themselves, that the world has always been in existence, implying that, it has an infinite past, and that takes away the standing of God as a creator and originator of all things.

However, the very same person believes in the reality of time and the existence of an eternal God. Now, for what purpose would that God have existed, if nothing on earth can be attributed to him? What right would he have, then to rule over the universe? It's either one of two positions, either there was a beginning to the universe, or that the universe had no beginning. To me, it's quite clear, if time is real, and we know it is, then, by the fabric or make-up of 'time', we can never have an objective judgement of its existence, let alone its purpose, if it's starting point was vague.

We might as well say that, time has no meaning. Let's take a hypothetical situation and imagine that we can capture an instant in time, let's call it (t) for illustration's sake, and we begin to traverse backwards, tracing its path as far as we can possibly go. We want to see where it came from. We start at (t) our captured moment, then we move to (t-1) the moment just before it, then to (t-2) the moment just before (t-1), and we go on like that. From the law of cause and effect, without going deeper into this analysis, we can safely assume that (t-2) is the cause of (t-1) and (t-1) becomes the effect, and (t-1) becomes the cause of (t) and t the effect.

In simpler terms, the moment preceding the other is the cause of that moment after it. It sounds confusing isn't it? But what we are doing here is simply trying to trace the movement of time backwards, going either minute by minute, second by second etc. as the case may be. So if we proceed like I have illustrated, and keep going backwards to the past; for as long as there is a moment before another, we can still attribute the existence of the next moment to it, and that shows we will still continue to go back until something changes. It's like subtracting one second from your age and keep doing that until something changes. Whatever was responsible for keeping me growing from stage to stage, keeps reducing in this scenario, until something changes, and that change emanates from a bigger source of life, which brought me into this world- my mother.

Now remember if this process goes on forever, without any change, then we have no 'time' to talk about because earlier, we argued for a beginning and proved that 'time' has indeed a starting point. So if we keep going backwards, we shall have to reach a point where it shall stop and there will be no previous moment to cause the next. At that point, something else and obviously, operating from outside of time, becomes the cause of that last moment in reverse, (which in actual fact is the first moment to exist) because nothing is without cause. This is the moment we shall describe in a few moments, when proving as to how God created 'time'. And that moment became the beginning of 'time'. This is what we read in the scriptures when they say "in the beginning" This is the beginning that they talk about. What makes it quite special, proving the beginning using 'time', is the fact that, the beginning of time was also the beginning of all things. Only time was privileged in that manner, and this says something about its positioning in the order of creation. It was the first creation, and everything else was then created inside time.

So besides the fact that scriptures support these views (of a beginning), several other fields of learning, have also come up with various explanations that confirm this position, and in those efforts; however, there seems to be overwhelming, even, scientific evidence in support of 'a beginning'. It appears; there is convergence of minds concurring on that view. That alone, permits us to confirm the existence of a beginning, because, "In the mouth of two or three witnesses shall a matter be established" It seems to me, that those who have chosen the contrary opinion, appear to be in a dilemma. Making that choice, in essence, rejects the notion of a creator completely. And that's what we referred to earlier as autonomous man. On the other hand though, supporters of the 'beginning' do not necessarily have to subscribe to the idea of a creator, although their testimony accepts the beginning. They ascribe their 'beginning' to other phenomena, separate from God. However, those who say the world has no beginning are faced with a predicament.

They seek justification for their choice in science, which agrees to a beginning, but rejects creation. Well and good, but their congruence with science is compromised again by the fact that, the evolution of science has more and more, resulted in scientific evidence, which supports that the earth itself and the universe as a whole has an age. Different schools of thought, within the discipline, however, emerge with different records of the universe's age, depending on their method in the determination. For our cause in this book, it is immaterial for us, to want to purse the most accurate age, though it would be desirable. It suffices for us to note that science has endorsed and vindicates the idea of 'the beginning', simply by its acknowledgement of the fact that the universe (earth included) has an age.

Not only have scientists accepted this, they also have experimental evidence to support their case. The generally accepted age of the earth and universe is around 4.55 billion years, although other scientists believe that the universe is way much younger than that. This then seems to bury the view that the universe has no beginning. If then science is the basis of those who reject a beginning, then unfortunately; clearly on this particular, but significant point in this matter, there exists the conflict, because science is pointing strongly to a beginning. The only problem according to me is what science then attributes to the event of the beginning, which they call the big bang, which is their point of convergence with the autonomous man, but that is a topic for another day. For now, let's celebrate that we both agree, on the reality of a beginning. It goes without saying, that if a beginning existed, then at a certain point after the passage of the time, an end shall come.

Again, there is congruence in the universe concerning that point. Where a beginning is established, an end becomes inevitable. So besides the fact that even scriptures support that view, from logic, we can also conclude the same. Now that we have argued and proved a beginning, then what was the precise moment of that beginning? I want us to go there now, and answer that question. But I need to give a bit of relief to the mind. I want to speak briefly on a topic, which I consider, very important but often overlooked or disregarded by people as they plan their time. After this discussion, we go back to answer that question about the beginning.

Chapter 10
Your life-long plan should not be done in isolation

Proverbs 1; 19 So are the ways of everyone that is greedy for gain; which taketh away the life of the owners thereof.

Proverbs 10; 2 Treasures of wickedness profit nothing: but righteousness delivereth from death.

The penalty of acquiring any possessions of life, by unfair means is the maximum possible punishment for a human life according to the scriptures, equivalent to that of murder. And for that reason, I thought it prudent to discuss that matter as it pertains to the way we acquire our time from another. While it is desirable to take action that ensures that you save, multiply, increase or preserve your time, care must be taken so that, such action must never be taken using unfair means or use of undue influence. Whatever method you employ, it must consider the impact on other people's time. Indeed, there is a thin line between robbing someone's time and effectively managing your own, and this line can easily be crossed without realising it, and that's why we bring up this topic at this point.

A time-conscious person must always plan his time giving regard to the next person. When we plan for our time, we should always remember we don't live in a vacuum and whatever method we decide to employ, it should take that into account. Several writers on the topic of time management offer some very useful and fantastic methods of time management, but often forget to give us the limits to which we can justifiably apply those solutions. They don't tell us how far we can go. There are also some scenarios, that we should address, where you do not necessarily have to rob another person of their time per se, but you simply manipulate or abuse it. It means you have created conditions that make it difficult for that person to access his time and plan objectively for it, for instance, when you show up late for an appointment.

In this chapter, we shall look at a few examples of all such, and examine when we might run the risk of crossing that line, and we try to offer ethical advice for consideration.

The fact that there is often more to do than we can possibly accomplish in the time available, and yet time cannot be stretched to accommodate everything; It gives us the motivation to try to preserve, save, increase, etc. our time and where possible use it to our advantage. Inasmuch as we would like to do that, it must never be without ethical considerations. No time planning can be truly successful without giving regard to the effort of another person affected by your plan in making theirs.

As a general rule, **Always trade value for another's time that you use to your advantage.**

In this section, we shall look first at a corporate setup, and examine the stages followed in the Time Scheduling process, as a generally accepted business method of effective time management. We start from identifying corporate time, delegating what can be delegated, prioritising what is left after delegation of tasks and then allocating time to the priority tasks in the scheduling stage. As we go through this process, we seek to show the ethical side that should receive attention and considered as part of our grand plan to managing time. Also note that to the extent that you employ these tactics on a personal level, you must also be guided by the same values we prescribed for the corporate.

Corporate time

The consequence of the scenarios described above is more pronounced in institutional setups due to the nature of the relationship between employee and the organisation. If you recall we said that an organisation compensated its employees for their time which it assumed power to control on employment. Right there, the company has the obligation to reward its employee. Upon signing up employees the organisation should remunerate them fairly. The company assumes control of their time and exploit it to its productive use. At that moment, the employee has no rights to his time, as it now will have assumed a new and legal identity which we are calling corporate time. Excessive control of the person's freedom and time without fair compensation for that resource could easily

This may begin to birth new challenges for the organisation, such as degenerate into a form of 'time slavery', resentment, retrogressive behaviour, etc. that would result in further loss of the already scarce resource. On the other hand, the employee has a duty to respect the fact that by agreeing to be employed, he has, in essence, sold his time to that organisation and is obliged to offer his best service during the period for which his time is demanded. You cannot offer your time to an organisation and at the same time want to employ the same elsewhere. That is the reality, and the ethical fact to be respected by every employee. So corporate time becomes the resource owned by the company, and which it avails to its employees to use in arriving at its goals.

Delegation

One of the well recommended tactics of managing time for a senior manager whose span of control maybe wide, is delegation. Upon a careful assessment of tasks, the manager may identify a motivated young manager and delegate some assignable duties, to release some of his time for more involving tasks or to allow more time to a crucial strategic project of the organisation. The results of this delegated authority will still be credited to the senior manager as this task is officially recognised by the company as his. However, what happens to the young manager's work load who most times will take on this new task without any kind of audit to ascertain his ability in terms of time to handle it.

It may mean that his own job suffers. A good manager should exchange value for the time offered by his subordinate. While he benefits from the time availed to his service by his junior, the manager must as his ethical and moral duty, also provide conditions that ensure that this young man benefits or learns a skill he would otherwise not have learned had he not offered him the chance.

The experience should be such that, it leaves him with better managerial capability and at a better standing in the organisation than his counterparts. In other words, the process should lead to a situation that promotes cross- functionality within the organisation. It means the organisation in promoting time efficient systems is at the same time developing and nurturing multitalented young managers capable of performing across the boundaries of their job descriptions.

Prioritising

The mark of a true time-conscious person is their ability to perform and perfect the art of prioritising his workload. The more one gets acquainted with consistently performing this act, the more proficient they are in executing their duties. The results are often very commendable and progressive. In the case of the manager, after assigning whatever he is capable of delegating, whatever remains on his list of tasks should be subjected to this process. The purpose of all these efforts is to avail more time to more crucial issues of the job. Having delegated some of his work and lessened the burden, he will still find that the available time will still not be enough to cover all his pending work, and that's when priorities have to be set. By prioritising he determines those things that he wants to make sure are done. Knowing what is priority is really the secret of gaining control of his time schedule. Consider also that in setting those priorities he does not stifle also the efforts of others and interfere with their work and efforts to contain their own.

In other words, the company time management systems should promote a culture of Mutual Support across the organisation. In this case, the time management systems foster a culture of shared values company wide. So in prioritising his time, there are three crucial considerations to make.

1. Ranking tasks by importance to your job and performance indicators
2. Ranking tasks by Urgency of the task

3. Ranking tasks by importance to company objectives

Importance, measures your desire to meet personal objectives for the job and company objectives at large, and Urgency relates to where you allocate it in terms of time. It is also important to note that importance and urgency do not always correlate. There are tasks that can be very urgent, but not very important. It's not surprising to find that such tasks may not make it onto the time schedule of a well - considered time plan.

So your time schedule should always, as far as possible reflect the importance you place on your objectives and how soon they must be done. It means the greater part of your schedule should consist to a larger extent of important things, and it is these that will determine your better rating during your time-related section of your appraisal.

Scheduling

After going through all the above stages, it is now time to actually commit your priority activities to time and this is the stage that completes the scheduling process. In reality when a matter is given priority and falls within the 'important' category during the prioritising stage, procrastination creeps in. You will discover that your natural or automatic response to the matter keeps pushing the job to a 'more appropriate and convenient' time.

Eventually all other small or urgent but unimportant tasks take precedence and are accomplished ahead of the important work.

Now scheduling your tasks ensures that the priority list you prepared in the process just before is actually respected and followed. Scheduling is the step that brings out the reality that time is a finite resource. This step, now commits time in the form of a duration to the highest ranking priority activity on your list, then the next and the next and so on until all activities are allocated a time slot. Committing to the time schedule and performing the tasks as laid down on the plan will always make sure that the next highest ranking priority activity is next. This is what makes the difference between an achiever and a non-achiever. It makes the difference between a busy manager and a busy for nothing manager.

These 2 kinds of managers are found in an organisation and like we said before, it is the interest of the company to have a system to guide this process in order to get the best results from all employees. When a manager is working on a schedule of this kind, they should be as true to themselves as possible and be ready to tackle the difficult tasks. Going through the whole process, up to scheduling and then finding no power to execute is a disservice to one self. It is a betrayal and disregard of effort done by the 'younger' you. The result is a demotivated 'younger' you, who does not trust his older version to bring to completion what he initiates, and so, no one is willing to get anything done, in the end it is the 'older' you, that suffers because if it was an important task, it still had to be done.

By now, the motivation to do it is more out of anxiety and panic rather than being self- motivated. Respect your prior effort towards your goals always, and that way, you keep yourself motivated and avoid procrastination. And also remember that any step taken towards your broad objective(s) is never a waste of time.

Other ethical and moral considerations

Respect other people's time

As you implement your own time strategy, do not forget the interest of the others that surround and affect your life materially. Your plan must to the extent possible accommodate or give allowance for people to interrupt and be part of your programme and in the same regard recognise the effect of your plan on their plan. Always remember that you are not the only person planning for your time. In fact, it is a good assumption to make that everyone you deal with has a plan for his own time. That puts you in a frame of mind that knows how to respect your own efforts, and the efforts of others. Always respect other people's time the same way you would have them treat your time.

That is the best way to establish your intention and be taken seriously. If only your time matters to you, others will find it difficult to support you. People can be your biggest enemy or impediment if you do not plan with them in mind. To those you can afford to do without, best to walk away from them and avoid your time interacting with theirs.

Need for speed

Ever noticed that one of the commonest methods of managing time is through speed? Indeed if you must manage time commendably, speed is a virtue. I would almost agree with the statement, that if you entertain thoughts of being a champion at managing your time and achieving great exploits, you need to have speed. This world has neither room nor sympathy to the slow. If you celebrate your slowness, and you extol that quality, it means you have subscribed to the idea of being second best. Someone faster shall always get there before you, even if you were the most deserving of the lot. I speak from experience and know that the lack of it, has affected my progress in life. If you are slow, I would like to challenge you.

Ask yourself this question. Of what benefit is it to me to be slow? If you are able to get at least one good reason, except being slow to anger, then I won't ask you to quit that behaviour, but I bet you, it's difficult to come up with good enough reason to be slow. So speed is a praiseworthy quality that everyone should be encouraged to work to achieve. But the interesting statistic about speed as a time management tool is that, it is the most abused of all time-saving techniques. Instead of it being harnessed to help keep pace with moving time, it's almost always summoned as a compensatory device. It always comes in handy when someone has already messed up. Surprising to note that even the slowest of people are masters of speed when it's needed as a compensatory tool. So speed is important, but inasmuch as we praise it, it must also be done with restraint.

Remember in an earlier chapter, I promised to reveal the person who kept using invisible brakes, as I stepped on the gas? By the time you finish reading this paragraph you will know 'her' identity. You just need to use your deductive skills. Now that scenario used to be a common occurrence in 'our' car, because......, yes, you guessed right, Speed! And speed not out of choice, but as always late for church, school, work, etc. If speed is used without due care, it violates even your beloved, and lots of systems, some of which have been put in place to curtail it. If it goes beyond the point where even you are no longer comfortable to sustain it, then stop and reconsider your action. At times, if not most, it is not worth the commotion, it takes you through. If it makes you and your acquaintances uncomfortable, and restless, it's time to adjust and prepare to deal with the consequences of arriving late, finishing late, etc.

Human Multi-tasking

Generally this refers to the ability of a person to handle more than one task or activity at the same time. At times we are faced with situations that leave us so swamped with pressing obligations to the extent that it becomes apparent to us that no matter what magic, speed or whatever technique we may employ, the demand for our time still remains too high. The work load is too much for the available time, but everything has to be done regardless. Such times call for action in the form of multitasking. Depending on the significance of the tasks at hand, you may need to, as quickly as possible go through the scheduling process described earlier in this chapter and establish priorities. Remember all this is happening outside a formal setting, and so it may not produce as accurate data as a formal time scheduling system would do, but the important thing to note is that, time 'scheduling' is a prerequisite for beneficial multitasking.

On one particular week, I was invited to speak at a seminar. At the same time, I was battling with a deadline for a personal project very dear to me. That same month I had enrolled for a personal development program that had daily exercises, which also included audio conditioning in addition to other tasks. I also happened at that time to be chairing an investment's project meeting with former classmates, and the discussions were happening over a social media platform, as a group. This was before taking into account, my normal daily routine of bathing, taking kids to school, attending to their home works, etc. To be frank, I was overwhelmed. I had to go through the scheduling process, unknowingly though, prioritised the activities, suspended some temporarily and scheduled those that I would tackle. During that week, I learnt the value of careful scheduling and multitasking because I had to carefully choose activities that I could tackle at one go so that I could fit them all in the available time.

Tasks such as bathing and the audio conditioning were combined such that as I bathed I also listened to the daily recording of my personal development program. There was not time to waste to the extent that I scheduled all e-mail and other social media commitments to times when I sat on the toilet seat.

It might appear as though I am being funny, but it certainly worked for me. To this day I practice multitasking in a systematic way. Those that criticise multitasking as a time waster should first learn the process of scheduling. That way the possibility of misalignment on combinations of tasks is reduced. Multi-tasking can have disastrous results if in the combination of tasks each will demand a high degree of concentration from you. For example, your daughter in her early stages needing your attention to monitor her reading, at the same time, you also want to be writing your research findings for your dissertation. For best results with multi-tasking, the combination of tasks need to have a significant amount of difference in concentration levels required by the mind to process each task efficiently, as even research has shown the challenges, that the mind takes on when processing data during multitasking.

Now, if one of the tasks in your multitasking effort includes the involvement of another person, be sure to be transferring value in that interaction, otherwise it becomes a deceitful act. If for example you stay with an elderly person, and they demand a good portion of your precious time by calling for attention and need for company, instead of having him sit and talk the whole time, while you pretend to listen meanwhile, you are concentrating on other things on your laptop.

That whole experience may not be so beneficial to both of you. As both do not really feel the satisfaction of the interaction. The old man feels ignored, and you feel disturbed. You would rather schedule a time slot for him, in which you multitask and perform an exercise that allows you to give him maximum attention possible while at the same time you are using your time progressively. You may, for instance, decide that the time be meal times. Make sure during meal times you call him and eat together and have vibrant discussions. After the meals, it's back to serious business, excuse yourself and work on your laptop.

Travelling Time

In this era of fleeting time, characterised by too many important tasks, and limited time, you want to make sure you make use of any idle time available. For example, each time you sit in a car, bus, and train, etc. or whatever mode of transport you use, travelling from one place to another, you actually have before you, time for free. You can choose to make use of all your travelling time, no matter how small to turn it into productive time.

In my earlier story of my busiest week, I also allocated some special activities such as responding to mail, texting, and research over the Internet etc, to travelling time. I entirely removed such tasks from my office routine and reserved them for time during travel, and it worked for me. I use that technique always, and since I discovered its value, I prefer to use public transport so that I release my time for productive business. I can bear witness, to the level of profitable business that has come to me and initiated through this method.

As you take advantage of your travel time, be mindful that you also consider the interests of others you travel with. This method can easily turn one into an antisocial being, which is not a desirable and acceptable trait. Other people actually receive medical treatment to correct that 'condition'. So make sure that you do not train yourself into becoming antisocial. Another consideration as you try to salvage idle time from travel is the effect that your method has on fellow travellers. Are you not disturbing their peace and infringing their space by your gadgets? All that has to be taken into consideration.

Borrowed time

Another source of potentially dead time is the time we spend waiting. As we wait, for whatever we are placed in a waiting queue for, still precious time does not wait, it keeps ticking. With this persistent shortage of time, you want to take advantage of any chance you find to find idle time and convert it to production. Waiting is a normal practice of life and happens every so often that its contribution to time loss in one's life cannot be ignored. So if it can't be ignored, we are better off planning and strategizing for it. And the best way to do it is through borrowing the time and using it for something else beneficial, in the meantime and while we wait. Another way one can take advantage of this kind of time is by keeping a book close by. Reading is one quality that would have made this world a better place by far. If people appreciated its value, certainly this sort of time would be better used by many.

As the name implies, borrowed time, just like anything else that is borrowed must be returned. Once your turn to be attended to has arrived, you return it back to its intended use. It should never be exchanged for an unintended purpose. If that was to be allowed to happen, it simply would have meant changing the purpose of the venue (the waiting area) to something else. It was by design and is our intention to end this section with this aspect. If you were observant, you would have noticed that this chapter sort of looks misplaced, but I intended it that way first to emphasis borrowed time and more importantly to get a breather from the heavier stuff of previous chapters. Now that we are done, we want to give the time back to the discussion of the beginning and so at this time we revert to that.

Chapter 11
But if we say that God created 'Time', when did He do that?

Indeed, we have no obvious record of such detail, but we know that, from the instant of its inception, (the beginning), as we have been convinced, it has never receded and is in full operation to this day. We encounter evidence of its operation in everyday of our lives, and we are sure of the fact that it was created, and that God created it, because we concluded earlier that, anything, that came after the beginning, was created, and that, only one authority was responsible for that occurrence. We even traced it back to its source and still came back to the same answer. **John 1; 1-3** supports this truth. *In the beginning was the Word, the Word was with God, and the Word was God. The same was in the beginning with God. All things were made by Him; and without him was not anything made that was made.* He is the ultimate cause of all things.

So now, the question of proving when He did it becomes necessary and it is our burden now to satisfy that quest. Well, I believe we have covered enough ground by now to attempt answering this question. Before we proceed, let us pause for a moment and concede that the Creator is beyond our comprehension, He is the Almighty. I am not saying this to cloud my explanation in mystery, and then seek solace in the same clouded explanation, but rather to warm you up to things to come. The character of this Creator is mindboggling, and there is need to prepare you for an extraordinary demonstration of His awesomeness in the actions that He took as He went about the creation business, as we are about to see. Creation is an exhibit of the qualities of God's nature, which clearly reveals His sovereignty over all things, and which, if deeply thought through, would eliminate any doubt, in any freethinking mind about His Omniscience. The safest, answer we can perhaps give to this question, (above) and get the approval and support of the majority of people would be to say, God created time at some point during the creation.

I also believe it to be so and of course with good reason. For a start, nowhere else after the story of creation, do we read of another stage when God had to re- convene for creating anything else again? In any case, from logic, it would not make good sense anyway to talk about the creation of time after the creation of any other thing because the beginning of 'time', was the beginning of all things. And further, 'time' is that which established order and change in the universe at the moment of its inception. So it could not have come any other time apart from the beginning. However, I am not sure, the extent to which this answer satisfies the questing. If this answer is considered good enough, I would submit then that the supplicant had no real intention to query. However, for those like me, not yet convinced, let's agree to demand more and come out of the 'safe' zone by attempt to look for the concealed, and deliver a more satisfying answer.

If only we understood the foundation upon which time was built, we would better appreciate its peculiar behaviour and elusive character. If just asserting its origins seem so difficult, how much more would be trying to comprehend it? There must surely be a mystery which mystery today, must be unfolded. The secret lies in the way it was created. It must have been a special type of creation. I am sure you don't recall any instance, during the narrative of the creation, when God commanded 'time' to come into being, do you? No! And because indeed that command was never given. So, how then did it come to be? Well, as we are about to validate, now, 'time' must fall in a category of God's creation that was not spoken into existence. Meaning to say or it would only leave us to conclude that there must have been other means that God also used to create, apart from speaking. Because we all agreed that all things that came after the beginning were created, and that qualifies 'time' to belong to that group of things. However, nowhere do we read or hear of its creation, but we know it exists.

It stands to reason, therefore, and justified too to confirm that time was created, and by 'special' means. ***Colossians 1; 16*** quoted above seems to give a hint in that direction. It lists classes of abstract things that it confirms as having been created by God too. The scripture is silent though about when it was done; how it was done; why they were created and so on? It just asserts their source. So these categories of creation exist, whether or not you have evidence of their creation. The senses that God gave to us enable us to behold his creation. However, by good reason, I believe he also made things that outwit those senses. That's why we battle to comprehend some of them, like 'time' for instance. It also implies that its creation method was somehow different. God had no need to speak them like He did for the others because, unless you were operating at His 'level', the evidence of His commands to create such would have eluded our perception. In reality, they became what He commanded them to be, but as for mankind, nothing physical was available for them to perceive, as evidence of their creation. Hence our belief that God chose to create them in silence. Thus 'time' only came into existence by God's inference.

In other words, time started to exist as a consequence of a particular deliberate act of God during creation, the act was meant to achieve a particular purpose, as stated in ***verse 4 of Genesis1, And God saw the light, that it was good: and God divided the light from darkness***. However, the 'residual effect' of that act of separating light from darkness resulted in what we now call time. Put in another way, God created time deliberately, but 'sub-consciously' so to say. Let's qualify this statement, because it may not sound proper to talk about the sub-consciousness of God. God in His sagacity knew that, the task He had to perform was to separate light from darkness, (referring to the above scripture) but, at the back of His mind also knew that creation of yet another thing would follow.

When God created light, an unimaginable atmosphere became. This (atmosphere) became the first ever recorded spectacle in the universe creating the excitement I would liken to the one experienced when events such as the solar eclipse, total eclipse, lunar eclipses, etc would occur. Only that, for that particular display, there was only one witness, and it was God Himself. The rest of us at best can only imagine. Now imagine the interaction of light and darkness; two powerful contrasting forces, coming from two different domains; the created, and the ancient. Take note that at that point, the operation of time had not yet started, and hence anything that existed at that moment could not have changed. They were both caused by a Higher Power to co-exist in the same space and at the same 'time' (for lack of a better word).

The period of this co-existence, is immaterial to us, whether it was an instant in time, or it took several years; it still does not change the fact that these two forces cohabited at some point. That will suffice for our explanation. I imagine that, the interaction of the two forces was not harmonious. Any slip up by either party, would have meant the extinction of the other, probably forever. I would suspect that darkness; was at the greatest risk under the circumstances. Because even from simple science, scientists confirm that darkness is the absence of light. However in this case, darkness stood its ground. The two great forces, meeting for the first time, in their lives, confronted each other unyieldingly. It had to take God Himself to break the deadlock. Later part of *Verse 4*; an alternative version of the verse would say, *He separated the light from darkness*. Take note; the separation, meant that none of the two had given in, to the other. If any of these two forces had succumbed, then the later part of verse 4 quoted above would not have been necessary. However, because that part of the verse exists, this points to a serious deadlock, a standstill, an impasse, which I liken to a great chronometer, awaiting the switch to be turned on. He then separated the light from darkness.

That act of separation, by the Almighty, was a significant point in the history of 'time'. The switch had been turned on. That instant of the separation was the beginning of time, and change was introduced into the universe. God in exercising His Authority over creation, then ordered safe domains for the two adversaries; light and darkness, using that which he created out of them, - (time) and (change), to guarantee perpetual existence of both. In other words, God gave dominion to 'time', to rule over light and darkness and set boundaries for their appearance in the universe. To this day, they all religiously obey this authority. Each was apportioned an appropriate share, taking turns to appear each day. It was by design. What an insightful God! And hence *verse 5 of Genesis1* is vindicated, *and God called the light Day, and the darkness he called Night. And the evening and the morning were the first day.* That which enabled evening and morning to come, had been established. The rest of God's creation which followed, then began to operate within the realm of time. The rest of what we are now going to discuss became possible. The platform for them to happen had been set. So let's now examine the other outstanding features of time and draw some lessons from it.

Lesson 1.
Maintain Balance in budgeting your time

Time is a great teacher; the environment described above reflects God's pleasure in observing balance. By its nature, when light appears, darkness must vanish, but he allowed them to co-exist. Each was necessary as a reminder to the other of the need to strike a balance. He then found a subtle way to separate them in the process coming up with 'time' which ensured that the balance was maintained. In the diverse missions we encounter life, if this aspect is not respected, our purpose on earth may be difficult to achieve.

Wherever time is to be managed, in whatever circumstance, be it personal, be it business, always strike the balancing act. It is crucial to a beneficial and purposeful life. Allocate necessary time to all activities that perpetuate your purpose. If God had not cared to take that precaution darkness would have disappeared off the face of the earth. It is critical to note that it was an act of precaution. That means it was deliberate. So as you plan your time, take the deliberate action to always strike a balance otherwise you may 'kill' necessary 'evils' in your life. In a nutshell, budget your time.

Ever wondered why dawn and dusk mesmerise humanity so much? I think; it is because those two occupy a space that almost resembles that spectacle witnessed only by God. I think God Himself saw how charming and wonderful that environment must have been, and so for the benefit of 'those' that did not have the privilege to witness this event; He ordered the appearance of these two pictures twice in each day. As sure as dawn heralds a new day, so does dusk, a new night.

Lesson 2
Make use of dusk and dawn to prepare for your day-and- night activities

Prepare for your new day at dawn, prepare for your new night at dusk. Don't start preparations for activities of the day, well into the day, and for night well into the night. You will lose out crucial time meant to enrich your day and night. These two distinct periods of life are special, and each has specific and special demands. You have been given these two periods to plan for your time. Once the day comes it heralds new things. You put yourself in a place of disadvantage by having a late start to your day. Starting early and preparing for your day during dawn produces wonderful results for your days' planning. It ensures that all important tasks have been allocated a well thought out portion of the days' time. Planning in this way puts you firmly in control of your days' activities. In itself, it is self-motivating. Dawn and Dusk are platforms of preparation often ignored but with amazing results. Consider making use of them each day, and see the wonderful results.

Special attributes of time

Chapter 12
Time was the first 'creation' to be conferred with dominion.

From the above discussion, we can begin to infer that starting from those early moments, 'time', started exercising some form of authority; I would put it that, in fact, it was the first creation of God that had dominion bestowed upon it. Again, we can logically, conclude why this dominion was not pronounced, or spoken upon it, as was the case when God pronounced dominion upon man. We know, and we have now come to understand that there was no instance, when God commanded 'time' into existence in speech, yet we know He created it. By the same reasoning, the authority or dominion, granted upon it, had no justifiable need to be mentioned. It was given and simply had to operate 'silently', in the realm in which it was created to act, and proof of its existence was witnessed as 'time' presided over its first subjects; light and day as we have demonstrated earlier. As we proceed, you shall discover that the domain covered by 'time' grew bigger, than God had initially intended. 'Other' creations, as we shall see later, gave up their right of dominion over it and handed it over to 'time', to rule over them too. We shall not discuss that at this moment, but keep it in mind until we tackle the issue.

We now know; that creation was done in different dimensions or levels and that the product(s) of each dimension or level, had to be attuned to its (their) own realm. Again, referring to *Colossians 1; 16*, Take note, that among the things that were created; dominions were also among them. Now, if dominions were created, the motive must have been to introduce order within its sphere of operation, because its effect was to confer authority on one thing, and dictate submission to that authority on another. We know that from the moment that time came into being, order was immediately established throughout the universe. Light and darkness gave way to each other as day and night responded to its authority. By what power, could time have done this? What right did it have to control other creations?

Why would other creations, submit to its presence? I put it that no order can ever be experienced, no matter the realm, if dominion is not established there. So we can confidently assert that dominion was bestowed upon 'time' by God, and must have been given right at inception, because it had to immediately assume such conferment to be able to exercise that dominion for it to be able fulfill its purpose.

So 'time' became the longest serving creation with dominion. The mere presence of it, in its domain, represents its supremacy over its subjects and that relationship is spontaneous. When man, appears anywhere, within the domain in which he was given the power to subdue, there is no need to announce his dominion. By instinct, animals and fish and birds and all other things mentioned at the conferment of man's authority just submit unprompted.

Lesson 3
Avoid surrendering your authority
In chapter 2, we established a law of Time conferred Authority. Where we said that time bestows this authority to the one who demonstrates a high regard for it over the one who does not. It is from this dominion as described above that time exercises such power to confer that authority as stated in the law. Dominion can only be passed from an authority. We concluded though, that this kind of authority, (time conferred authority) is relevant only at the point where time matters arise between the two individuals concerned without regard to location.

First mention of 'dominion' in the scriptures was in verse 26 of Genesis 1 and there, God was speaking to his 'Others.' Let us examine the scripture a little and see if we can come up with anything fascinating.

As we do that, keep in mind *Colossians 1; 16*, and take particular notice of the things that this verse suggests as having been created. Now, back to our scripture, *And God said, Let us make man in our image, after our likeness: and let them have dominion over the fish of the sea, and over the fowl of the air, and over the cattle, and over all the earth, and over every creeping thing that creepeth upon the earth.*

In the situation God, reveals or makes a declaration of intent. At this point, we can judge that man was not yet created. However, God's intention to equip 'him' with dominion was already announced to his council. I am persuaded therefore to believe that by that time, dominions had already been created because in his dialogue with His 'Others,' he expresses His desire to create man, and also shows His intention to equip the man with dominion, which the scripture in Colossians confirms to be among those things that were created, but which up to this point gives no clue as to when they were created. However, we see here in this scripture, that God already wanted to use it (dominion). Which causes me to believe that at that point when God announced his intention dominions were already in existence. God could not have intended to use something that was not yet there. In the scripture, he does not even command dominions to come into existence first so that he could use them, but speaks as if knowing they already were there. Even in verse 28 when he then pronounces or commands man to possess it dominion, there is no mention of its creation. As we follow the narration of creation, we appreciate that, God never created anything before its purpose was established and due. You will realise that nothing that God created can outlast its purpose. Purpose dictates inception and culmination of a thing. Meaning that, dominions had already been created before man, and on the premise of purpose, must have had to fulfill another purpose(s), because God operates on purpose, which proves, first of all, that even though first mention of "dominion" in the scriptures was in reference to man;

man was however not the first creation to receive it, and this lays good grounds for our argument that 'time' must have been indeed the first, because the latter part of the verse goes on to suggest the 'size' of man's domain. It would seem that all the things which we read as having been created before the man was created were all placed under his dominion. However, nowhere in the description of such things do we infer that time was among them.

The significance of the conferment of dominion on man in verse 28, is that it allows us, to appreciate and interpret the meaning of the word. Why is it important? It is important because, we have established that 'time' was the first creation to receive dominion. It is, however, only in this verse now that we first encounter such a conferment in speech during the whole creation. We can only conclude then that the 'meaning' of the 'dominion' given to time, earlier as we have shown, over its subjects, naturally carried the same meaning as did the one granted to mankind over his own subjects. As we now appreciate, nothing concerning 'time' was ever mentioned to hint on its creation, but evidence of its dealings abound in the universe. Let's put it another way if 'dominion' meant authority and power, for mankind over, his subjects, then we may as well, say, 'time' also, has authority and power, over its own subjects. I put it at this juncture, that 'time' has dominion in its domain the same way man has it in his. This leads us to a very exciting question, and we deal with it in the next few moments.

But who has dominion over the other between the two?

What better way to tackle this question than to go back to the time when both these creations of God first came into being, but this time to explore their relationship? The day that man disobeyed God the creator; was the moment that ushered in conflict in creation including the weighty conflict between man and 'time', because that 'fall' disturbed the perfect plan of God for His creation which God had placed entirely in man's domain to uphold. If man, at some point, had the mandate to uphold the plan of God for his creation; then this suggests that, before that event of the fall, man had dominion over time. The choice to live or to die was squarely dependent upon man. The equilibrium that existed in the universe before the event of **Genesis 1; 6,** when man 'fell' before God, was interrupted. The command of God in verse 3 of Genesis 1 was like a dangling 'key', the significance of the choice taken by the man would define a new relationship where man would become subject, rather than a master of time. That point in history is so significant to this discussion, because it is the point, when man handed over the keys to 'time' forever.

It was the first time that man had to exercise their special God- given privilege of free-will. At that point our fore-parents made a choice, which essentially guaranteed our relentless attempt to race after time, because in exercising their freedom of choice, by partaking of that which they had been ordered not to, they activated the curse of death, which effectively set in motion the clock that numbered the days of a man's life. If you had the privilege to live forever, like they did, there would surely be no merit in racing against time as we do now. Why would you have to? However, the consequence of their decision, endorsed the beginning of a limited life. Imagine the panic, once you realise that you are going to die soon. In reality, 'time' becomes your biggest enemy. You begin to realise just, how much you have to do before you go, and believe me, the task is almost insurmountable. So from that day until the end comes, unfortunately, man became slave to 'time'. We shall revisit this issue at a later stage to shed more light on this relationship, for now we will stop here.

Chapter 13
Time is the most obedient creation of God.

Here we will need to cover a lot of background before we get into the actual work of defending this assertion. Can we really say obedience to God is a trait worth applauding? Is it of substance, to be an obedient creation? Let alone, to carry the tag of being the most obedient of them all. Has it ever occurred to you, that 'time' is the only creation that has never lost time, in pursuing its purpose, and since it was one of the first things to be created, it has certainly outlived most if not all of creation, yet of all things nothing is more resolute? It has traversed its whole life from that moment of its inception, to this day without losing a second of its 'itself'.

'Time' is exactly where it should have been by now. If at all, it ever got stalled, even for a moment, God himself would have caused it. However, as we shall see later, even He has chosen never to interfere with its operation. Does it not also seem so true, that the gap between where you are today, and where you should have been, is covered by a trait, which time has mastered better than you? Time! just obeyed God and does what it was created to do. It simply ticks away and never stops. This is what made 'time' the universal standard for all existence, explaining why everything else is benchmarked against it. I don't know if the same can be said about man.

Lesson 4
Our Sub conscious is our best available option
The basis of our prescription in Chapter 4 of employing the mind, more specifically the subconscious mind in fighting the battle against time, is in direct response to this attribute of time being obedient. If we teach our subconscious mind to account for every moment that passes in our life, we stand a better chance than to want to consciously confront it.

When the sub-conscious mind takes over this task, it means we won't have to think about being conscious of time. Responses to matters pertaining to time will be an automatic action. It is genetically coded to perform such tasks that do not require your conscious involvement.

Where do you find yourself today, in relation to where you should have been? How do you account for the gap in between? The gap insinuates that time must have been lost somewhere, and that lost time can be traced back to an act of 'disobedience'. Can't we say now, that obedience has some merit, which demands our commitment, and ought to be a quality we all hold dear?

However, if we talk about obedience, it must of necessarily be a response to a summon, which causes it to happen. Hence the question; obedience to what? Well, I would like to think that obedience always responds to 'purpose'. If purpose is known, then responding to its call is easier to obey. So then, does everything have a purpose?

The purposefulness of creation.

In pursuing our 'obedience' assertion, let us now interrogate purpose. We will start by asking this question - "*Did God bring the creation into being to fulfill a predetermined purpose or plan, or was the creation brought into being without aim or plan?*" Answering this question is necessary to prove purposefulness, which, if proven, will provide a yardstick against which we can gauge level of obedience of any form of creation, in answering its call. If we succeed in proving purpose in the whole of creation, then we are better placed to make the comparison that led to the assertion we have made, that 'time' is the most obedient of all creation. We do hereby seek to defend that position. Whichever creation it be that would emerge as being true to its purpose, testifies its obedience to God who established and assigned it. In this book we insist that 'time' sticks out as the most obedient of all creation and that's why it is in step with God's purpose.

Before we even summon the support of scripture to attempt the above question of 'purpose', it should not be very difficult to persuade an objective mind just by mere observation of the complex systems of the whole universe that; this dumbfounding work, regardless of what you consider to be its cause, is indeed, a masterpiece, and the stroke of a genius. The consistency, the degree of coherence and cohesion in the universe are proof on its own, of well calculated thought and predetermined purpose for every entity that exists in it. The logic, with which these systems function; points to the work of a 'super mind', which supposedly, thoroughly thought through, made necessary considerations, and emerged with a balanced, and perfect universe. Surely there must have been a 'superior mind' imagining things beyond even the imagination of humans, free from the influence of error, and exercising supreme authority over all things. I imagine, that this greater power, had no need to learn and that's why up to this day, even with the sophistication and great strides in technology, we are yet to provide answers, concerning what.

'This force' created, unaided. Technology as we know it, has improved the quality of our lives, and assisted humanity in unraveling some of the mysteries of creation, without which; we would never had come close to scratching even just the surface. So now, imagine how much the humans have had to invest in 'learning' and the time it has taken just to unbundle what this 'great power' was able to achieve without the benefit of the same. This speaks volumes of the depth of knowledge released by 'this power'. The fact also that humans are the only creature who's learning abilities have managed to decode some of the inventions of this 'great mind' with commendable determination gives a clue as to the nature of this 'power'. It must surely have possessed some form of humanoid persona. So humans somehow, flowing from this discussion must be a lesser form of this 'thing'.

Remember also that all findings, discoveries and researches being carried out now are all in retrospect. In other words we are working backwards from the answer. Why would we have to research so much, putting so much resources into it, if it was that simple? It certainly takes much less faith to believe that some 'higher authority' took deliberate action to purposefully place all things, each, in their rightful space, and, with a precise assignment to carry out than to say the universe just occurred on its own. And further suggest that the occurrence originated from nothing and that all things just existed by coincidence.

What about: all the evidence of careful thought abounding and obvious throughout the universe? The logic with which the universe operates? The origins of life itself? The purposefulness of the existence of anything? The obedience of creation in answering its call? What better motivation to exist than to operate in intended purpose? I would say, if purpose is fulfilled, life is fulfilled.

If we insist, that a coincidental event just happened, leading to all the things that we see today, how then could 'coincidence' possibly epitomise the precision we witness? Okay, let us give 'this coincidence' the benefit of doubt and 'just agree' that, it caused creation. The question now comes, what is 'coincidence' if all things caused by 'it', work in perfection? Let's pause another crucial question. If before this event called 'the Big Bang', there truly was 'absolute nothingness' as they say where then was the 'huge potential' stored that would become 'something'? The reason, why the Big-bang theory falls short in my view, to justify its validity, is that it is based on improbable and unsupported foundations whose basis is flawed. An attorney at law, will tell you what grueling a task it is trying to defend and sustain a lie, and how overwhelming and enduring and stubborn the truth can be.

The experience of life has taught us that the life of any structure depends heavily on the foundations upon which it was built. No matter how decorated the structure may become, if foundations are shaky, the structure is not free from the threat of collapse. Although science has widely accepted this theory, as the best possible explanation for the existence of the universe, they do accept, however, that it is packed, with 'material' contradictions and violations of very fundamental laws of science. Well, it's tough reality for scientists I suppose, because an alternative explanation had to be provided, since science should never be founded on faith and the supernatural, but rather on empirical evidence, which can be tested and proven.

This, however, brings us back to our initial query, when we first questioned 'coincidence' moments ago. Is it not these very attributes we alluded to earlier, which give relevance to the discipline of science? The consistency of the laws of the universe; the logic of things; the origins of life itself, and all such things as mentioned earlier. Science would be meaningless if coincidence or chance, rather than purpose, was responsible for creation. What logical result or outcome would be expected from a coincidental or accidental creation? But why are we talking about this anyway? It is important to prove beyond doubt, that all things have a purpose and owe that purposefulness to something. If a thing has a purpose, you cannot run away from the fact that the benefactor had an interest in creating that thing. However, if we can't prove purposefulness in the universe, then even a creator is not necessary.

But surely someone, must have been thinking, and it must have been a 'big someone' for that matter, who was responsible for all this! As for me, until I get more enlightenment to the contrary I shall hold on to my belief and reiterate and still declare that God almighty took care of business during 'The Creation'. And from our discussion above it would seem quite clear that each piece of creation was put in its place to serve a particular purpose.

Before we even go down to the specifics of individual assignments given to all creations, scriptures say, *'Thou art worthy, O Lord, to receive glory and honour and power: for thou, hast created all things, and for thy pleasure they are and were created'- Revelation 4; 11.*

Much earlier in the book, we alluded to the fact that all things were created by Him, and even now we still emphasise that point and now wish to justify it. From this scripture, we understand that, God found pleasure in the act of creation. That is why, in the first chapter of Genesis, during course of 'The creation', He paused at every completed piece of work and reflected on it and expressed His pleasure. Take note also that nothing that did not meet God's expectation of perfection for His purposes made it into existence. Each time that we read in the book of Genesis that God created, and looked in admiration, and saw how good it was, confirms to us that He had been satisfied enough to give, His seal of approval and rewarded, whatever it was, with existence and the abilities to perform its assigned tasks. This is to say that God's creation was complete and perfect in its founding.

Genesis 2; 1 sums it all up, *'Thus the heavens and the earth were completed in all their vast arrays'.'.* With this knowledge, we can safely conclude that all creations were endowed and decorated with special attributes and unique abilities that allow them to play their part in justifying their existence, thereby glorifying God their Creator. We could go on and attempt to describe the purpose of every entity in the universe but certainly this is a task that no one will be willing to attempt, because firstly, God Himself has not revealed all things to us.

Some things remain mysteries in our present life and secondly; this would definitely be an assignment for eternity, unless of course you were created for that purpose. Need I remind you of the last portion of the verse immediately above, 'in all their vast arrays'. It sums up the measure of immensity of the whole 'systems'. So let us agree here to concentrate only on 'time' for now and try to understand the purpose for which God created it.

Lesson 5
Purpose is key to managing your time effectively
Throughout the initial stages of the book, we have emphasised a purpose as being the key constituent of a well-managed time in one's life. In fact, on the guidelines for our strategy to managing time, it is given as a prerequisite. Knowing purpose is the best way to sidestep the whims of time, because whatever you undertake to do on earth, as long as it conforms to your purpose can never be a waste of time, even if it's misplaced in its timing. So again, I say discover your own purpose.

Chapter 14
What was God's purpose in inventing 'time?'

What would it mean to have a world without time?

In this book, we shall attempt to explain the purpose for which 'time' was created. There is definitely no way we can ever exhaust this question because of the enormous amount of work bestowed upon this creature but we shall try to do enough though, at least to enable an understanding of the gravity of its purpose. As we get into this very arduous task, I shall ask you now to fully engage your mind and all necessary faculties into deep imagination.

What could possibly limit this creature?

Before I started putting this piece of work on paper, one question lingered on my mind - "The spirituality of time." I kept wondering if 'time' could be classified as a spirit because to me, it behaved as though it possessed such qualities. I understand now that the word 'spiritual' on its own connotes life, and that being the case it presupposes a vessel which carries the life. If a vessel cannot be found, the spirit is limited. In other words, a spirit can only operate in a physical body in this realm of humans. It is a rule of this earthly existence; and as we have already seen the laws and systems of this existence are amazingly consistent. That means the laws hold true each time they are called to action. So if time was a spirit, it too had to obey this rule without exception. So, on that basis we can safely reject the possibility of a spiritual operation of 'time'. Further, we know that time does not have any other precondition apart from God who established it.

Lesson 6
Acknowledge the role of the Creator

This is the basis upon which we advise the acknowledgement of the role of the Almighty in trying to craft a plan to win time. What better way to understand something than to consult the inventor of that thing. If you side with the inventor of any useful thing, you are bound to get a better understanding of it rather than by any other means.

It attained independent survival from other creatures, upon its creation. That's why, no matter the kind of occurrence that takes place anywhere in the universe, that cannot sway the operation of time. This is indeed a special attribute. That means, time will not at any moment, be dependent on any created thing, in order to function. The same, however, cannot be said for any other creation in the universe. The existence of anything else depends on the occurrence of one thing or another. In other words, nothing else is without cause.

If the statement, that, 'time has no other precondition apart from God', is true, then we can see for sure, how an attempt to influence time becomes a difficult task. Because possibly, what good reason can you give God who knows all things, to stop, delay or manipulate time in any way? Now suppose, that the vessel ceases to exist, the spirit will stop functioning until it finds another place to operate from. However, time has no need for a medium to operate from, and so can never be interrupted or inconvenienced by anything, as long as God has allowed it. That need for a working platform, seems to suggest that a spirit is only confined to a specific location at any given moment. But tell me of a place devoid of 'time', does such a place exist?

Even in spiritual realms like the heavens, where God is believed to live. Scriptures support the belief that it exists there too, and is observed, just the way we do here on earth. *Revelation 8:1* makes reference to 'time' operating in heaven.

People may come up with different interpretations of what the 'half hour' may mean but the fact that a duration has been established is evidence enough to conclude that time exists even in heaven. Another common explanation, for existence of 'time' in heaven, is music.

Scriptures confirm also that music is a dominant feature of heaven. What is music without time? Remove time in music, chaos erupts. The one fact that seems to be coming out so strongly in all this is that, time can almost be described as omnipresent. Even a scientist cannot talk of any space anywhere in the universe that is completely devoid of time. Its integrity is intact universally.

Lesson 7
Time affects every person the same way, regardless of location

Keep the same values of managing time wherever you find yourself. Its nature and character are never changed by your location. By being confused and relaxed about its state and your management of it, when in a different environment contributes to the waste of it. Refuse to be confused and stay resolute and determined.

Any other thing, in the universe, can be proved scientifically or otherwise, to respond to a change in their environment. Water, for example, would freeze as it approaches a cold region, and becomes vapour when subjected to heat. This confirms its inability to resist changes to its surrounding environment, under different conditions. Light is known to change its behaviour, particularly its 'speed' when it enters different mediums, such as glass, air, water, etc.

So, if something; which is not seen by the physical eye, and does not need to be compelled by anything that is in the universe to happen, and is unhindered and cannot be limited to a location; and remains the same, wherever it is found; we can conclude, therefore, that 'that thing' possesses superior qualities, the likes of which, none other possesses. It cannot be classified as a spirit, because its functionality is not hindered by location or any other thing for that matter.

Chapter 15
Time has a Spiritual Mandate to fulfill

Although we have quashed the notion of time being a spirit, or operating spiritually, we now seek to prove that, it, however, has a great spiritual mandate to fulfill, which according to the scriptures, was bestowed upon it by God, before the foundations of the world. We know that God has blessed humanity with lots of spiritual gifts. Amongst them, is found, the gift of salvation. I concur with the many great men of God, who consider this gift to mankind as the greatest gift of them all. The unfolding and manifestation of this great gift, had to be revealed to the intended heirs, (the humans), in order for them to receive and embrace it. The 'gift' could only make sense to these lesser beings, if it was revealed to them in an environment that they would understand. The all-knowing God then chose that this revelation be in a realm which operates in time. Remember at the time of these thoughts, God existed in a realm with no time. So, 'time' was not an accident, or an afterthought. It was a deliberate act of God. Earlier, we said, 'time' was a consequence of certain actions of God as he was going about his business of creating. It was a 'consequence' with purpose. It was perceived by God in his thoughts, and then established on earth and beyond to fulfill His plan.

Imagine waking up one day and there was no time, but everything else being there. What kind of atmosphere do you picture in that environment? It is possibly an unconceivable idea, but let's try to picture it anyway. Do you realise that; that atmosphere would necessarily resemble living in eternity, and yet human beings do not possess the attributes required to comprehend such an existence? We know that only God dwells and thrives in that kind of environment. So suggesting that it would become possible for man to live as God does, even for just a moment, is asking for too much; especially if that status quo is to obtain here on earth. Earth was not designed to contain eternity, and that's why we struggle to comprehend it. Albert Einstein, a great scientist, in one of his works on what is called 'Relativity Theory' also made suggestions, to that effect, and was supported by many other great 'spirits' in science, that 'Time' was only an illusion. His suggestion pointed to the idea that, we live in eternity. Even though it was said by Einstein, or had it been said by any other authority in science for that matter does not qualify it as correct.

I still maintain that God could not have had such a plan for the human life. To me, 'Time' is a stubborn reality, of this life. It cannot just be an illusion. It exists and functions by purpose. While you still debate on that, let me now bring forth an argument which would rest this case. God himself, would oppose the existence of such a set of circumstances, (time not being there) and with a great passion too, for the following reasons: First, and obvious reason, would be that, it simply was not part of His plan. That reason alone can be sufficient to settle the matter, nevertheless, for the sake of those of 'little faith', let me attempt, to go deeper and try to satisfy them. I know you are certainly not one of those, but I want you to just read on and enjoy.

Now, let me take your mind back to the time before creation. I need to be sure that your imagination has taken you back to that era. Before anything ever existed, scriptures say, God already had plans in His thoughts, for all His creations, mankind being at the centre of that plan. He specifically determined, to 'set apart' humanity through the sacrifice of His own son, as *Ephesians 1; 4 - 5 confirms. According as he hath chosen us in him before the foundation of the world, that we should be holy and without blame before him in love: Having predestined us unto the adoption of children by Jesus Christ to himself, according to the good pleasure of his will*, Keep in mind that we are still at that time before anything was there.

Now, if God had already, so loved humanity before the foundations of the world, and in His foreknowledge knew that one day because of disobedience and sin, He would have to justify us 'somehow', and He decided, that this justification be through His son, Jesus Christ. He surely knew, at that point (before creation), how He was going to execute his plan. *1 Peter 1; 20, tells us that "Who verily was foreordained before the foundations of the world, but was manifest in these last times for you"* (All this was happening back then)

This verse, first confirms what the earlier verse says, and secondly, also brings out, yet, another intriguing idea. It addresses the question of God's choice of the time, when 'this ransom', shall be revealed, and not only that, but also sheds light on why he chose that specific period, and that it was for our sake. Why was that important? The scripture has made it clear, that God had a choice, of when to reveal the ransom. He could have done it, at that time by Himself and still achieved his goal; I believe. Remember all this was done for His pleasure and will. So nothing could have stopped Him if he had so wished.

But He chose not to bypass our concerns, as humans, because He viewed us as interested parties, and found pleasure in involving us to take part in His plan. If He had decided to go ahead with His plan without us, who would have believed Him? It would not have been necessary actually, for Him then to go ahead and create people, because the purpose of the gift of salvation would have become meaningless. Because this would mean, creating already saved people, and besides, how would he choose whom to save? Because it is a personal choice. Wouldn't that have justified the idea of predestination? However, in his plan, each of us had to live and better 'his own time' to work out his own salvation.

Now, if you are following well, you must have figured out by now, that this ransom, was God's own choice, to redeem humanity, then **Hebrews 9; 26**, discloses that, the ransom, shall appear at the *end of the world* to put away sin, by the sacrifice of Himself.

This scripture makes reference to 'that ransom', as confirming what we have already established, but it also brings out, a new and significant insight. It hints on the possibility of some kind of passage of time from the one revealed in the last verse. Those words 'at the end of the world' presuppose that there must have been a beginning somewhere. And remember we have already argued in favour and concluded that there was indeed a beginning. Further the verse reveals even more precisely, that the appearance of the ransom would not occur at the beginning or in the middle, but towards the end of the world. If we want to relate these three periods, (established in God's mind before creation) to our common understanding, we can easily classify them in the following categories; past, present, and future. Because these thoughts pertain to us, we can even to go further and try to locate ourselves within that timeline. Now from logic, and even from our description of the beginning, our existence can no longer be classed in that era.

Lesson 8
Locate your progress on your timeline
In Chapter 2, we presented a table, dividing the life of an individual into three categories with distinct periods and characteristics. That strategy was copied straight from God's own strategy for his planning and time management. Locate your progress on your timeline. Do an earnest assessment of progress on your milestones and revise your strategy.

How much of your journey have you travelled?

We got a big clue from the last scripture, that even the middle era is gone past us. It says the ransom shall appear at the end of the world, and as we stand today, the ransom has already been and not just, but quite a while ago. That means, the greater part of the journey to the end has already been travelled. The plan of God for humanity and his creation is nearing its fulfillment. However, let me get you out of the current and take you back again to the time before anything was there. The question then comes, what is it then, that would occupy the space between the beginning and that end? Or let us ask it this way, what is it that would separate these distinct eons? If the intention of God was that this would happen in eternity why then was it necessary for scriptures to define these 'signposts'? Moreover, remember that all this was still happening in thought, but still had to be fulfilled in the physical, which was still to come. Without a physical manifestation, God's thoughts would never have been revealed to us - the intended beneficiaries of those thoughts.

And finally, when all is said and done, God shall prevail over- all things. In-fact scriptures say that God will become all in all.
1 Corinthians 15; 28   and when all things shall be subdued unto him (subject all things under him) then shall the Son also himself be subjected unto him that put all things under him, that God may be all in all. That will be the end of all things. And note also that this comes after the 'ransom' has appeared. This clarification is necessary because the first scripture said, the ransom shall appear at the end of the world, but that does not mean the end has come. Still, more, will come after that, which shall endorse the end, and which is what we have just read in the verse above.

I am aware, that I have loaded you with a lot of scriptures, but allow me now, to explain. The scriptures above are a summary of God's plan for all His creations from *before the beginning* of the world, to the eventual end, which, by-the- way is still to come, though not too far from now. We may live to see it, if God allows. As we might have already observed, the most predominant beneficiary of this plan, for his creation is humankind.

It seems, or it would appear that the whole plan of God *subsists* specifically for their salvation. This shows you how purposefully God placed mankind in the hierarchy of his creation, and the priorities which He assigned to them, above all other things. The thoughts that follow will definitely change the way you view 'time' from this moment on. If you looked at all the scriptures immediately above, you would begin to appreciate that the mysteries and secrets of God's thoughts before the foundations of the world about his whole plan were meant to be revealed in 'time'.

In other words, time provided the 'stage' for God's thoughts to be made manifest to the human mind. If you carefully examine the scriptures, in the order which I presented, which, by the way, I took time to place in a careful sequence which follows some chronology. You will notice that there is a progression of events in the meditation of God, from the first verse to the last. Somehow we can begin to appreciate that some kind of a Time-Line was established in the mind and planning of God, well before time itself was created.

Lesson 9
Learn from God, The mind is crucial in time planning
It has to start in the mind. Well before you get there, the plan for your time has to be already established. Visualise the timeline in your mind and take steps to actualise it. As you do that, keep in mind that your thoughts and their manifestation are separated by time.

The span of the Time-line established in God's mind covered the entire life of creation. You will also notice one common striking feature in all these scriptures. Remember, we said that this is the summary of the whole plan of God for His creation. Each of these scriptures, reveal two distinct positions: the initiation of the divine ideas, and the manifestation of them. By their intent, these two positions could not have happened at the same time, because God knew that it would be too heavy for mankind to comprehend and was too loaded to be contained simultaneously. Imagine that, God's thoughts for His plan abridged the entire life of the universe well before it's time. The fact that, all these thoughts occurred before the beginning of the world, and that, their manifestation had to happen in that 'place' (the world) which was not yet, should be proof enough of their fated separation. What was going to provide that separation? It only makes sense to conclude that whatever it was; it had to be a medium which could facilitate the unfolding of those thoughts into 'reality' for all humanity to see and comprehend.

Again, we witness and testify to the homogeneity of God as He went about doing his business, because earlier we discussed that, when confronted with a similar situation, (during the creation of time) where two forces could not share the same space, (light and darkness). God brought that which he had perceived in his thoughts much earlier and created it and summoned it into action to separate them. It is also interesting to note that by the same principle, He separated his thoughts and their manifestation, using the same medium - 'time'. Talk about consistency. Is it not interesting to note that in both scenarios, the two things that had to be separated in each case were coming from different realms, i.e. realm before creation, and that after? Time fitted perfectly to fulfill that desire, and so the unfolding of God's thoughts began when time started. This should show you the weight, that this phenomenon (called time) possesses in God's view, because, it brought meaning (to us) to His whole plan.

Lesson 10
Learn from God the chief strategist - His plan covered the entire life of the universe.
The big idea of this book is to have a plan for managing your time, but do not end there. Go further and say the plan should span your lifetime. So let's make it clear. Your strategy for time has to cover your entire life.

This should not come as a surprise because we have just demonstrated in the story of God above that he did exactly that. God's plan for time spans the life of the whole universe. Just as we have advised earlier, that along the way, your plan should be punctuated by milestones or sign posts. It is important to know that, the advice was extracted from God himself. His plan is open for all to see. The coming of His Son was yet another milestone in his plan for his time. We have lived a few thousand years after that milestone, and we know that we are closer now to the end, than ever before. We can trace his plan and be able to figure out where we are now. Don't delay further, find your purpose and plan for your time now. If God planned for His, how much more ought you?

That 'weight' referred to above, however, does not come in defense of the contention by others, that 'it is God who needs time, not 'time' that needs God'. Take care not to confuse the status or importance of time. As some might say, 'Time' is the power that enables God to fulfill his purposes. That is not the case, God did not and does not need time, because before it was there, He already existed without it and was self- fulfilled. This line of argument falls short, even by just the explanation of the premeditations of God concerning His plan.

He thought about it, before even creating it. Can we say then, that, if the creator or inventor of anything, finds it necessary to include something in his invention, to enable an outcome, then that thing becomes the power through which he is able to fulfill his task? I disagree. Even when he created it, he chooses when to operate within it and when to operate outside of it. His mysteries had to make sense to the human mind and so God devised a way that mankind would understand and see the events of God's plan unfold to the day when He shall subject all things to Himself. So time was created for mankind to perceive and to bring meaning to His word. If God had not found it necessary to create time, He could have opted for other means, to do the same job as it does.

All He needed was something that would bring meaning to His whole plan and that the intended beneficiaries would comprehend it.

Taking it from another angle, if God had not created 'time', the foundations upon which faith is based would be challenged. God is so serious about faith to the extent that without it, He can never be pleased. I doubt that He would allow a situation that causes Him displeasure, when the whole essence of His creation was for his pleasure. Faith is relevant only when time appears, and works, as it were, to elude the barriers that time imposes. The kind of environment without 'time' would render the scriptures meaningless. The book of Hebrews as an example, especially Chapter 11, which talks about faith, could safely have been condemned as worthless. As Faith and hope will have no meaning. For you will have no need for 'hope'; because hope, speaks of things to come, and yet you already are there, where the things to come are, because you already live in the future.

There won't be such a thing as 'things not yet seen' because things not yet seen exist somewhere in the future, which future, you would have already embraced. I am not sure, the extent to which you appreciate the concept of faith and hope, but as far as I am concerned, if this scenario was allowed to exist, that is to say, if time, was given the freewill to decide when to show up and when not to, then, we would hop in and out of eternity as 'time' pleased. The absence of it would plunge us into eternity and the reverse would be true if it became present. More importantly, the whole story of Christianity would crumble, because there was no platform for humanity to work out their salvation, which we have shown as the priority of God in His planning. The coming of Christ to save humanity was an act of faith, and even the salvation we received through Christ is an act of faith. The whole life of a Christian should be grounded in faith, otherwise; it will all be in vain. For it is impossible to please God without faith.

Colossians 1; 27 talks about Christ the Hope of Glory, but if hope has been rendered useless, then what is the point in following Christ.

Lesson 11
Why God created time.
The whole discussion we are having of God's grand plan was designed with man in mind. At the centre of all these initiatives, God sought to pursue a relationship with humanity. He intended to bring them back to Himself by the sacrifice of His Son. This was the real story behind everything else he did. If by the time you finish this book, you haven't grasped anything, make sure this point you don't miss. The theologian we quoted earlier actually said, *'The importance of the improvement of time upon other accounts is in subordination to this. Thus if a man, by anything he hath, may save his life, which he must lose without it, he will look upon that by which he hath the opportunity of escaping so great an evil as death, to be very precious.'*

All the time management techniques we are learning here will have no meaning whatsoever if we lose the plot. This is the real essence of the whole plan of God. Time was created as an opportunity for humanity to escape eternal misery. If you fail on all else but achieve on building this relationship with your maker, you have made an eternal inheritance for yourself. Personally, I choose both. I prefer to live a fulfilled earthly life and also inherit God's eternal gift of life with Him. That is where the spiritual mandate of time lies.

Even the promise of living in paradise for eternity with God would become a useless promise without 'time', because eternity would already be present. There would not be any incentive or motivation for humanity to strive to live a righteous life in order to receive a reward at the end of life. That means, evil would flourish and chaos would abound on earth.

God is Holy and detests evil, so surely this (timeless world) could not have been in His plan. His predetermined original plan for the universe persists even to this day, and we are all witnesses to this, because we exist and operate in time.

He has fixed time to occupy a certain space in the universe to perform its duty as it was instructed when it passed into existence. If the absence of time, would mean existence even in just any one of the above scenarios, as we have seen, that would throw God's plans and purposes into chaos, like we have tried to demonstrate here. There is no way God would have allowed His word to be taunted in that manner. For His word is worth much to Him and He would defend it. We have this assurance that God would not be put to shame by a failing word because of who He is and His unfailing promises. He cannot afford to be a liar.

He cannot taint His own reputation. I am sure you too can appreciate how important 'time' must be to God. If it is this important to God, how much more then for us, considering that we have established, that humanity is or was at the centre of God's plan in His creation? And that it is us who operate within its confines. It must mean that it ought to be esteemed highly by mankind. It wasn't created for God; He created it for us, so that we would fulfill His plans and bring Him pleasure.

Chapter 16
Time has a physical mandate to perform.

Let me just take one more scenario, before you disengage from your imagination mode. If you were given a book and told that it was a very exciting book, and that you should read it. However, you are told that the 1000 paged book has the same contents on all the 1000 pages, and you also discover that it is indeed true. Firstly, what value would you assign to that book? Will the production cost match the value of the book? Do you find it logical to produce such a book? Well, let me leave you to think. You will probably have even more questions to ask than answers. So, what are we trying to say here? I trust you will agree with me that a clever person will read page 1 if they have to, and close the book.

You read that page; you have read all. The other 999 pages have no incremental value except to increase the volume. I also trust that you agree with me that if you read page 1, you are as good as the fool who is going to read all the one thousand pages. What would be the unpropitious 'quality' that would discourage anyone from reading the book from cover to cover? Remember, we said, time is that which introduced change to the universe. If the universe was created without 'time', then it would have remained as it was when it was created. It would exactly resemble a page in the book, which ever page you choose. That means, what was, would be what is, and what will be. Let me briefly take you away to the scientific world of physics. Long ago, during the times of Albert Einstein, physicists developed a philosophy they called space- time continuum.

"This concept regarded 'space' as consisting of three dimensions, (length, width, and height) and time as consisting of one dimension, which became the fourth dimension of space. This concept was developed after a series of experimental physics which proved that

space and time could no longer continue as separate entities as they had always believed, but had to be combined into a physical entity which they called space – time. Experimental evidence, supported by mathematical equations of relativity displayed that both space and time coordinates of any event must get fused together to form this 4-dimensional Space-Time continuum, in order to accurately describe what we see. All events, places, moments in history, actions, etc. are described in terms of their location in space - time. (what is s-t continuum?)" Einstein.stanford.edu

We can see, here that, even science rejects the possibility of an eventful space existing separately from time. In simpler language; if anything is to take place in the universe, space and time have to interact. So, even science supports, that time had to exist first in order for any kind of change to happen in the universe. The picture of the book resembles a universe without time, where no change will occur. I trust that at some point in your life; you have had to pause for a photograph. Ever tried to think what you will be doing? Let me tell you, in case you didn't realize. What you will be attempting to do there is stopping or freezing time. So, the outcome of that act, is an environment without time. That is why nothing will ever change on that picture. The person pausing for the picture is aware of the reality, that any moment later, will represent completely changed circumstances, and hence we want to capture the now position. Does it not click to you, why it's always the best moments or best looks that we love to capture? It's because we realise that we have stopped time and wish to live in our best moments forever.

Now let us answer those questions we asked about the book earlier; certainly, there would be no value to assign to a universe in a state of perpetual pause. It is what we may refer to as a white elephant. Relating it to our own lives, the fact that it is an elephant is encouraging, just the colour has to change, and if it does, it will change its fortunes. The work done during the production (the creation) and the cost incurred would not justify the end product. Why would God create such a magnanimous universe that would look the same from the first day, to the last day? That means no change will occur at any point in the universe because time was not present as a dimension of space. It's too much work for very little reward.

I cannot figure out the purpose of creating such a meaningless object, so full of promise and full of eternal potential. If there is some dormant potential hidden in you today, get up, do something about that potential, or else you are as good as the one without it.

Lesson 12
Eternal potential is useless
Once one has established their purpose, the hidden potential that supports the purpose will begin to emerge. Even before purpose is established, inherent potential can still be observed in an individual. If you don't get up now, to put that potential into productive use, you are just as good as those not so privileged with such talent. Your advantage can't be taken advantage of. So for what use is the advantage? If ever the expression "he/she is so full of potential "is used on you. Let that be a challenge to you and remind you that there is something you have not done. Never take that as a compliment, even when it's meant to be.

The logic of creating such a work would be questionable, because its usefulness is doubtful yet so much has been put into it. A waste of resources, I would say.

Special qualities of time

All these situations and imaginations we have created have been an attempt to prove the value of time as a resource for God, man, and the entire universe.

I don't doubt at all that God has placed a high-value price tag on this special creation. You will appreciate from all the above circumstances what humiliation; God would have suffered if for some reason, time had decided to disobey Him. Certainly, God would not have afforded such to happen. I am also convinced that with all the credentials it possesses, the consistency with which it has performed its assigned duties and the loyalty it has demonstrated in service to its creator and master, surely, God would emerge with good testimony for this amazing creation. He would appear in full defense of its tenacity in executing its mandate on earth. In fact, I can boldly throw a challenge, and assert that, no other creation of God comes close in obedience to God and in fulfillment of purpose and mandate on earth than time, not even mankind. We have shown how it is a big component of God's ultimate plan for His every creation. I take it this justifies the reason as to why 'time' has been highly favoured by the creator and adorned with special attributes and qualities, which mimic His own. The next few paragraphs will show the special 'shared' qualities. Remember we are still trying to demonstrate why time is an exceptional project by God.

It goes without say that God possesses the most amazing qualities we can ever imagine. No one and nothing can ever possess the full package that He enjoys. In fact, the attributes that we ascribe to Him are only those that are known to man. I believe we can never exhaust God. This is what separates Him and makes Him, God. However, in His infinite wisdom, He has allowed His creatures to share in His perfection as he chooses for each one of them. Science cannot explain God, because even as He shares his qualities with all creations yet He himself is not subject to depletion. He remains the same. A source that cannot be exhausted. Any quality ever displayed by any created thing, draws from this source, and is apportioned and given according to its purpose for His pleasure. Time is no exception. Like any other creation, it has been granted qualities that allow it to be effective in its own domain(s). Every-thing is unique in its own making and purpose, and has been equipped enough to effectively perform its assigned duties. The qualities though, that God has bestowed upon 'time' are really special, because for those specific ones, only 'it' and Him possess such and as such performs special assignments. It also explains why time is a difficult subject to tackle. And even the confusion surrounding 'their' relationship stems from this fact.

3. Time is omnipresent

We touched a bit on this attribute when we questioned spirituality of time. We eliminated the possibility of such an attribute for a spirit on the basis that a spirit was confined only to the location where its 'container' can function. Time, on the other hand, cannot be contained. It cannot be housed, or be restrained. No one can arrest it, to bring relief from its effects. No matter your location, be it at the poles, at the equator, in space, other planets, or any other place you may think of, time is there and will pass for you the same way it passes for anybody elsewhere. I cannot reconcile or imagine what a 'time-free zone' would look like, and how it would operate, without affecting life everywhere else. It is thinkable though, to imagine any other creation being absent in any given location or universe wide, and still have life go on. So this is yet another quality, peculiar to time and no other creation has the same privilege.

4. Time will outlast all creation

From that ancient moment on, time has persisted to this very modern hour, traversing epochs, periods, ages, eras, dynasties, emperors, kingdoms, even ruler-ships back then and those to come. We have seen how God made sure, and stood resolutely in defense of His word, more specifically His promises. From the scriptures we referred to, logically we can also deduce and conclude that time shall outlast all creation.

For we conceded earlier, that, any activity after the beginning, operated within the realm of time. Creation is enveloped in time. And as such, no activity in the universe can occur outside this realm. In other words, time forms the boundaries of all activities of creation. When time shall cease that will be the end of all things. But is it true that a time shall come, when there shall be no more time?

5. Time operates in all realms.

When God created the universe, he found it necessary to create 'territories.' He demarcated boundaries and made rules that would govern life in each zone. In each zone, He placed the rightful occupants suited to the conditions of the obtaining environment. He made sure that crossing those boundaries to escape to another, was not an easy thing to do. That is why, it is impossible for the inhabitants of one zone to sustain a prolonged existence or operate optimally, in another zone if at all they have succeeded to. There are life-supporting structures in the different realms that God created for the intended inhabitants in each zone. If an inhabitant of one realm escapes into the other, it is bound to be limited there, at best, but the most probable outcome is its demise. Only temporary transcendence is possible, but not without a price. Either a change of state in its being, or major modifications have happened in order to access life or existence in the foreign space.

Often, because whatever is meant to promote and sustain life in one realm may not be available in the other, the visiting inhabitant has to carry supplies of the life-supporting systems in order to make it there. The challenge I am pausing right away, to you reader, is; think of anything, that has thriven outside its ordained boundaries. In certain but exceptional cases, however, as in the case of human beings accessing heaven; certain preconditions have to have been met and upon fulfilling those requires a complete transformation of life into another form, compatible with the new environment.

I stand to be corrected, that apart from God, the only other thing, that can transcend realms, territories, boundaries, etc. is 'time', and does so naturally, without any need for any adjustment whatsoever. It is amazing that even in realms beyond, it's being; operation and identity remain intact.

Revelation 8; 1, confirms that even in heaven, it is acknowledged and applied the same way it is on earth. *And when he had opened the seventh seal, there was silence in heaven for about the space of half an hour*. What is this 'half an hour'? Is it a duration? If it is, is it the same duration we understand to be 30 minutes long here on earth? If not, does it mean there is a parallel form of time that runs there in heaven independently of ours? That being the case why is the statement not qualified? to say that the period referred to measures time according to the standards of heaven. If these scriptures were written for us, would it make sense for them to speak to us using parameters which we cannot comprehend? I am persuaded to believe that, 'that time' is understood there, the same way we understand ours here, and because of that, we can relate to it, and we can form an opinion in our minds of what that meant.

To this day, it is problematic to the scientist to bring tangible proof that time behaves differently in different spaces. In their theories of 'time dilation, and time travel, for example, their efforts are being frustrated and limited by the absence of real life, feasible evidence to prove that time is relative, and can behave differently in different environments.

For example, one need to travel in a spaceship, at the speed of light, in order to prove that time inside the ship would slow down in comparison to that on earth. So their evidence is confined to theoretical situations only, although the theories are sound on paper.

The greatest challenge faced by these scientists, is that their best effort to attempt an explanation is in the form of thought experiments, called paradoxes, whose feasibility for now is still beyond human capacity.

So we assert our position, with full knowledge of the scientist's reservations about our declaration, that time can traverse realms and remain relevant and operational, with no effect on it whatsoever. No other creation, to my knowledge can match 'time' in this regard.

Chapter 17
What the 'great minds' had to say about Time

We have gone far and wide, in search of truths, myths and mysteries about this super invention of God. We have talked about its complex nature and exclusive character. I am sure you can agree with me, that very few things if any come close to matching the qualities and abilities associated with time. It appears to have been loaded with limitless assignments to carry out throughout the universe, and even this book, cannot claim to have even scratched the surface. Be that as it may, it has shown great resilience and a strong 'life force' loaded with such powerful credentials that it will be a befitting conclusion to this book to interrogate its seemingly invincible nature. Can anyone or anything claim to have conquered time?

Ever since the 'fall' when humanity lost the privilege they had over time, and surrendered dominion in the process, man has struggled relentlessly, to try to reclaim his hold on time. All the energies exerted in this endeavour are testimony to the great resolve and determination by man to restore his dominion. Interestingly in trying to understand it and conquer it, it appears people got more confused and bewildered. Below is testimony of how mankind has tried to understand and explain it, but still ended up more confused. To make it even more convincing, the people we have selected are among the greatest minds ever to have lived. Just take a moment to reflect on what they said after giving it their best shot:

The confusion of giant minds in pursuit of its conquest

Sir Isaac Newton Conceded that it was too difficult a task to explain

Born in England in 1642, he was an English physicist, a mathematician and a great philosopher who is widely viewed as one of the most influential scientists of all time, and a key figure in the scientific revolution.

He made a spirited attempt at trying to uncover the mysteries of 'time' 'space' and motion, and came up with a commendable effort that influenced the works of scientists, even to this day. Although there were conflicting views about the true character of time and space, during those days, he became famed for what is now known as Newtonian Time, otherwise known as Absolute time. In putting forward his argument, he said, *"I do not define time, space, place and motion, as being well known to all. Only I must observe that the common people conceive those quantities under no other notions but from the relation they bear to sensible objects."* He then went ahead and defined the time thus, *"Absolute, true and mathematical time, of itself, and from its own nature flows equably without regard to anything external, and by another name is called duration*: He goes on further to distinguish his 'time' from Relative time, saying, *"relative, apparent and common time, is some sensible and external(whether accurate or unequable) measure of duration by the means of motion, which is commonly used instead of true time......"* in other words, he was suggesting that there are two kinds of time in the universe. One that was perfect and not commonly understood and another, which was common and bore a lot of inaccuracies. He believed in the accurate one.

In the later part of his life, he said, *"To explain all nature is too difficult a task for anyone man or even for any one age. Tis much better to do a little with certainty and leave the rest for others that come after you, than to explain all things by conjecture without making sure of anything.*

Albert Einstein believed that the universe was timeless
Born in Germany in 1870, a long way after Isaac Newton's time. He was a great philosopher of science and one of the greatest physicists of all time. His most invaluable contribution to the field of science, particularly modern physics were his General theory of Relativity. He is credited with the world's most famous equation $E=mc2$, for mass-energy equivalence.

This person was honoured with many prestigious awards in recognition of his immense contribution to the field of science, and was recently voted 'Person of the Century by Time Magazine for the influence he has exerted in the world. This is the person, who concluded in all his scientific ingenuity, that this universe is timeless. In his own words, *"Time has no independent existence apart from the order of events by which we measure it."* In other words, time only appears when an event happens, then we can start to measure it, otherwise it does not exist. He concluded that the past, present, and future, all exist simultaneously. He rejected their separation and marked them as unreal. When his friend Besso died, in a condolence message to his family, and to further assert this belief, he wrote, *"for us, physicists believe the separation between past, present, and future is only an illusion, although a convincing one."* His work was, however, a direct contradiction to theories propounded by fellow scientist Isaac Newton much earlier.

Aristotole argued that 'time' has no beginning or ending

You can imagine after dedicating a whole chapter earlier in this book, arguing for a beginning, Aristotle, rejected that. Born in 384 BCE in Greece. He was a Greek philosopher and great scientist and remains one of the most influential people who ever lived. He contributed to almost every field of human knowledge known during his day. Brian Magee, a British philosopher of the 20th century described him in these words. *"It is doubtful, whether any human being has ever known as much as he did."* As a man known to have contributed to almost every field, that means, he could not have missed a chance to talk about time. You will certainly find his beliefs to be very interesting, especially after you have read this book from the beginning. He believed that the universe has an infinite past, with no beginning. He argues that time has no beginning or end, and criticised the notion of a beginning of time as illogical. His words *"where time is, motion is. However, time had no beginning; for every moment of time is the end of past and the beginning of future time." "Consequently, there was no first moment. If there was a beginning of time, then there was no time before the first moment of time. However, this cannot be allowed; for he who says "before" indicates time past. It is therefore, impossible that time had a beginning."*

St Augustine Just could not understand it.

*B*orn 13 November 354 AD in Africa, Algeria, is believed to be one of the most intelligent men who ever lived. He was a great philosopher, and later became a Christian theologian whose works greatly influenced the development of what is called Western Christianity and Philosophy. Western Christianity makes up nearly 90% of Christians worldwide.

In one of his great, works popularised as 'Confessions', he wrote, *"For what is time? Who can easily and briefly explain it? Who can even comprehend it in thought or put the answer into words? Yet is it not true that in conversation we refer to nothing more familiar or knowingly than time? And surely we understand it when we speak of it; we understand it also when we hear another speak of it. "What then, is time? If no one asks me, I know what it is. If I wish to explain it to him who asks me, I do not know. However, I say with confidence that I know that if nothing passed away, there would be no past time; and if nothing were still coming, there would be no future time; and if there was nothing at all, there would be no present time.*

And the modern scientists!

Equipped with all this knowledge and materials gathered by our predecessors, the likes of those mentioned in this book and even many more others that have made great contributions in their various areas and whose impact touches our lives today but not mentioned herein. An era blessed with the privilege of perfecting those works that were started by such great fore-runners. It would be a great betrayal and a violation of the trust bestowed upon us as successors or heirs of such heritage if we failed to revolutionise and conquer the world. Well, this time without mentioning specific names, great scientific exploits are being carried out in laboratories of the different parts of the world. One of the most intriguing areas being studied by our ambitious scientists is the very controversial yet very fascinating subject of Time Travel. It is a scientific theory (for now), that suggests the possibility of unrestricted travel through time.

It suggests that one is able to travel through time to the future, back to the present and even back to the past, with the aid of a machine. The time machine works in such a way that it creates conditions that enable the 'fabric' of time and space to be warped into a loop that eventually creates the path which makes time travel possible. Wow! How about that for science? It means that one is able to travel to their past and alter certain parts of their past, to even change their destiny. Or even to visit their future and affect what awaits them there. It sounds very intriguing, doesn't it? I know that the temptation to dismiss these theories as baseless, is an obvious reaction. But hang on a little don't dismiss these folks just yet. To date, no scientific theory receives better acceptance in the field of 'time' and space than does the theories of relativity postulated by none other than the famous Albert Einstein. In fact, the whole time travel adventure is inspired by his works. The reason why, scientists are enthusiastic about working on this project is its theoretical possibility.

The concept is well supported by good and solid scientific theory and faces no material prohibitions in science. In other words, it's only a matter of time, and that is the attitude of the scientists working on the project. They anticipate that at the current rate of technological advancement, another century or just a few more centuries are required before we can begin to 'time travel'. Unfortunately for us, but those after us should really be privileged if it should go through.

In my research on this theory, and just for your information, I discovered something that fascinated me. Sympathizers of this concept have that much faith in it, to the extent that the idea of a time travel 'fund' has been mooted, and websites developed to start mobilizing the funds. Though the intention (of collecting these funds) may be questionable, it is quite interesting that they have takers for the product. Those willing to subscribe for the program will benefit from the accumulation of compounded interest on the invested amount, until the day when time travel becomes a reality. Whenever that will be, your investment shall be used to fund the time travel associated with your life, and sustain your continued existence. The key idea is that death does not worry you now, because they will travel through time back to the time of your death, change those circumstances that caused your death and bingo!!! You are back to life. This is real and happening in this world if you were not aware. Check the Internet for yourself if you wish to verify this.

Despite all the scientific evidence presented in support of this theory, and the seemingly good basis upon which it is founded, there exist serious, real limitations that threaten the attainment and subsistence of this concept. For a start, the resources, in financial terms, required to fund such an operation, are the greatest challenge. Millions of dollars are required just on start-up costs alone. Secondly, the time traveller can only travel back in time only to the point when the time machine was switched on. Thirdly, there are also certain paradoxes that many believe, make time travel impossible. Like the infamous grandfather paradox. Imagine going back in time, 200 years, you would emerge in a time before you were born and meet your grandfather, and you kill him. Now, in the flow of time, as we already appreciate, 'cause' precedes 'effect'. In this scenario, the effect, (you) emerge before the cause, (your birth), in violation of that law. So until the scientists are able to come up with methods to counter these obstacles, time travel may remain a dream for these ambitious men.

Having summoned the prowess of these great thinkers such as those whose influence and impact have transformed the world. It goes without saying that humanity has indeed been blessed to have communed with such special people. The world would surely not have been the same without the input of such outstanding capability. They did their part and very well, and left an enduring legacy. Today we can only marvel at what they managed to contribute to the world, during their time. The ones we mentioned are not the only ones, there are many more that we could have talked about. But owing to time, we could not mention them by name, but even so their contribution to humanity is much appreciated.

Now, if people of such mental power, and great influence could reveal their own short comings and strain in understanding this 'thing', how much more would it be for the ordinary man or "the common man"? in Aristotle's words. What more the modern scientists, battling to create 'super' technology that would subordinate time to enable 'us' to enjoy unrestricted access, back to our past and forth into our future. However, the obstacles they have to contend with are enormous. I am no scientist myself but just looking at the nature of hurdles they have to rise above, to come up with the kind of technology required to perform this task, personally I won't give them my confidence vote. It seems to me that kind of feat is beyond human boundaries. There should be a limit, to territories where man can successfully venture, and I conclude here, that this is one such area. The foregoing is evidence of its elusive nature and all the special qualities and abilities it possesses, makes it a creation of limited access to us.

I would like to conclude this chapter by quoting the words of Mark Rushdoony in his article the 'Theology of Time' who *says, "God decreed that man should have dominion over the creation, so our study of its science, when done in obedience to him and his calling, is a rewarding and fulfilling pursuit. When we seek to transcend our creaturely limits and seek by reason what we are given to accept by faith as a gift of God, we frustrate rather than further our understanding."*

Chapter 18
Are we destined to fail against Time?

There is no doubt, that when God created both man and 'time', He was aware of the consequences of their interaction. I say that for two reasons, firstly, recall that, before the world was even formed, He saw the end from the beginning, and obviously, everything else, in between. Again in *Genesis 2; 17*, the later part; says, *for in the day that thou eatest thereof thou shalt surely die.* Conditional verdict was declared. Note that, the verdict was pronounced before the act of the disobedience. God already knew the dynamics of this relationship. The forbidden act, once fulfilled, immediately caused man to become a mortal being, heralding the beginning of his end. The upper limit of his life instantly became established, and the lower limit became fixed. In other words, the day of his birth (creation) immediately assumed a new firm meaning, which it did not have prior to that act, because we can safely conclude that man was meant to live forever, and so that day had little significance.

After the act, an 'end' (the upper limit) had been caused, and of necessity, begged for a 'beginning'. At that moment, the duration of a man's life was established, in the eyes of God, and at that instant, man began to operate in, and governed by 'time'. From that instant, no man could ever live beyond the limit that was set for him, except of course when He, the supreme ruler of the universe allowed it. So we can safely say that if God was aware of these consequences, then He must have created the means to manage the eventual relationship, caused by man's decision. So we can see that the history of the relationship of these two creations of God is quite ancient, and He had an active part in shaping it. He did not wake up to the surprise of finding them together. He authored their relationship and created conditions to ensure that a harmonious relationship ensued. These are the conditions that we seek to uncover in this book, and to know how we can take advantage of them to in order to maintain harmony with time. Unfortunately for humans, or is it fortunately?

In the ensuing set up, God did not give us the privilege of being able to alter or affect the course of 'time' in whichever way. He obviously envisaged a chaotic world, if that had been allowed. Access to that closet required special intervention by God himself. He designed it such that, permission would have to be sought by man, and granted only upon His consent. In fact, He not only granted it, but made certain, that He would become involved in delivering it. We shall see sense of this as we proceed with evidence in scriptures. It became the standard that each time man was perceived to have prevailed over 'time', or had conquered it in some way or the other, would signify divine assistance. From that, we can almost always assert that God's aid precedes every event where man triumphs over time. But what is God's interest in all this? God is making certain that he directs your life towards and defending His and your purpose in this life. Let us see, if we can now support all this from recorded evidence.

If God had not found it necessary to rescue man from this callous brawl, man would have been condemned to eternal defeat, even to the extent of eternal destruction. Remember we are talking about the relationship between man and time. For it is how well, we fare against 'time' in this life, that determines our welfare, first, here on this earth, and more importantly, in the life after. Experience has proven that since the fall, God determined to stand in defense of man against time for His purposes to prevail, and there are several accounts in the scriptures where this was demonstrated. It should be a comforting thought for all mankind to know that God himself takes sides with us whenever 'time' threatens our existence or whenever there seems to be a life-threatening confrontation especially if 'purpose' is at risk. Just before we look at those scriptures, it would make sense for us to explain why we would need God on our side to face time.

Remember that at its creation, it had to take God to separate light from darkness - the act which we proved to be what caused 'time' to start ticking. Think of it that; when once a moment in time is gone past, it will be gone forever. No amount of effort can ever bring it back to our present reality. It will permanently claim a place in the past, and will have no portion whatsoever in the 'now' life. Even God himself has chosen not to deal with it in this manner, (trying to reverse it), not that He could not, but that He allowed it because it is He that gave it the command to 'pass'. So we ask, did 'time' ever really stop at any point during its existence for any reason at all, even to give way to man or is there an instant where time ever got reversed? Well, the scriptures we are going to examine now seem to suggest so.

I believed that many of us are convinced that the following scriptures are records or evidence of God helping man either to stop or actually reverse time for the benefit of man. However, after our discussion, I shall leave it to you to make a ruling anew. As for me, I am convinced, that time has never stopped since the beginning.

The first, *Joshua 10; 13, "…and the sun stood still, and the moon stayed, until the people had avenged themselves upon their enemies, Is it not written in the book of Ja'shar? So the sun stood still in the midst of heaven, and hastened not to go down about a whole day."* On this account, take notice that God showed up and stood in defense of man against time, but notice also that in his action to defend, He did not affect or stop the passage of time, but that He disturbed the routine of those things (sun, moon, etc) that He placed in the sky during creation, to be signs that marked the passage of time, according to *Genesis 1; 14*. Remember, these signs were hung up in the sky, after 'time' had already begun. This proves that 'time' had no real need of 'sign posts' in order to pass.

In fact, those were placed in the heavens for the sake of the inhabitants of the universe to make sense of the passage of time. This event made it appear to all who observed it like as if time had been stopped, simply by the fact that the 'signals' had indicated so. The interpretation that 'time' had stopped was an opinion of the observer, and not fact on the ground. But did it really stop? If the hands of a clock are caused to stop, does that translate to a stoppage of 'time'? You the reader could be the best judge.

The second instance recorded where it is believed that time was stopped, and not only that, but also that it was reversed by God, once again in favour of mankind , is found *in Isaiah 38; 8 Behold, I will bring again the shadow of the degrees, which is gone down in the sun dial of Ahaz, ten degrees* backwards. *So the sun returned ten degrees, by which degrees it was gone down.*

The lack of precise detail concerning the actual conditions and information relating to the gadget referred to in this scripture, makes the assertion of the actual reversal of time quite difficult to verify, but what is certainly undeniable about this event is that indeed the miracle of the retreating shadow took place as God had promised, with the resultant effect of a longer than normal day being experienced by those in that Land. To this day, no one can fully explain the real science behind this spectacle. Did the earth reverse the motion in its path or did it rotate backwards on its axis? Or did God just cause the shadow to bend backwards without affecting anything else? Or did time really stop and started ticking backwards? Well, these questions still beg for answers, but for now, what we can confirm is that indeed there was an extraordinary happening, that appeared to reverse the passing of time. All we have again, just like in the previous case, is the testimony of the observer of the 'signs of time', but the question remains, did it really stop? If you have been following well from the start, I am sure that you will agree that in both cases, evidence of time passing is overwhelming because the stoppage of the sun did not cause all other things to stop, hence change continued to happen elsewhere in the universe, and, on that premise alone, according to the knowledge we have so far acquired about time, we can safely rule out the possibility of time having stopped or even reversed. Remember we settled, that, change was a sufficient condition to establish the passage of time, and that time was a necessary precondition for change. I put it to you that during the moments when the sun stood still, the sword of battle did not stop; neither did the action in Hezekiah's palace and elsewhere. The cause of the stoppage in the first story was, in fact, to affect change.

In the second account, the contention that time stopped is further challenged and complicated, when we read that kings and rulers from neighbouring regions sent envoys to enquire about this unusual event that had happened in His Land. *2 Chronicles 32; 31*. If time had really stopped, even they, in their own countries would have witnessed it there, wherever they were. However, it appears from this, that, if indeed it stopped, then it only stopped in that particular region. However, as it appears in this case, everybody else in all other neighboring nations, did not experience this 'stoppage and reversal' of 'time'. Can we then objectively say that this event caused time to stop? How widespread was this experience felt throughout the universe. Again be the judge, just as I have already given you the liberty to infer over this matter.

It is in this same way that God intervenes in human lives even to this day to rescue them from the instincts of time. God uses the same principles He has always used, and that's why we found pleasure in studying how he did it back then. Let me put it this way, 'Time', is God's gift to humanity with a special call to accomplish. It gives Him great pleasure when His creation supports His purpose. When we talked about the purpose of time earlier, we emphasised that the salvation of mankind was the foremost concern on God's mind. Even before anything was made, as we saw, those thoughts really dominated His mind. The psalmist, mindful of this fact, and in a display of great awe, as to why God would single out humanity in all of His creations to be special, wrote: *"What is man that thou art so mindful of Him? And the son of man, that thou visitest him"? In Psalm 8; 4.*

We have seen how God intended for those thoughts to be revealed and made manifest to mankind. We have also come to understand that 'time' carries the spiritual mandate to fulfill that desire. Yet we realise too, that there is a physical side also, to man's life where the spiritual will find its fulfillment. Therefore, the physical also requires special attention, which must never be downplayed, because it is this which determines happiness or sadness both in the present life and after life of a human being. With this in mind, let us now turn to exploring the ways, in which man was meant to prevail over 'time' in this physical existence.

So in answer to those questions above, God enables us to stand our ground. Time cannot entirely have its way, with us as it pleases, although it has the potential. There are several interventions that God has designed, to 'soften' the grip of time upon mankind. If God had not found it necessary to invent these, men would surely have been condemned to eternal defeat without even a chance of ever recovering lost ground and would even fail to fulfill their earthly purpose. It is worth saying, at this juncture, that losing time is a natural process of a man's life, which is inevitable and most times, the causes of which are beyond what human effort is capable of averting. There is therefore, no need to beat ourselves too hard, especially, when circumstances dictate where we end up in terms of our time.

And it is for that reason that God put in place mechanisms to rescue the situation for us. Having said that, let me also hasten to make it clear; there is a distinction between lost time and wasted time. In his powerful sermon - *The Preciousness of Time*, Jonathan Edwards, said, *life in its entire duration is short, consider what you have already lost, then how short is it?*

God's mechanisms to rescue our time are meant to recover that portion of our time, for which we had no control in losing. For how then, would a just God hold us to account for what we had no power to change? Remember, at one point we shall all have to answer for our time. So for that portion of your time which falls under the jurisdiction of your power, make no mistake and employ it to the best use. Because it is that which shall cause you pains to explain to your Maker. The other portion, not to worry, God will find a suitable way of dealing with that portion to restore it to you. And having received the 'reimbursement', by which ever fashion, it's like a new lease of life, especially now that you understand its value to you. Let us now look at some of God's prescriptions for lost time.

Chapter 19
Time and Chance

One of the 'devices' or mechanism that was fashioned by God to deal with time, in a man's life, especially to put man in a position of advantage and recover lost time, is chance. In one of the sermons by my own pastor, he introduced this word, as it pertains to the word of God. In his own words, he said, "there are certain words we should add to our vocabulary, among them; the word 'Chance'." He referred to this particular scripture: *Ecclesiastes 9; 11 "I returned, and saw under the sun, that the race is not to the swift, nor the battle to the strong, neither yet bread to the wise, nor yet riches to the man of understanding, nor yet favour to men of skill; however, time and chance happeneth to them all".* I did add it, to my own vocabulary, and developed interest to study it further in order to understand what it meant.

So before we start trying to understand 'chance', allow me a little while to ponder on the meaning of the verse. Who knows, perhaps, we could even get to understand the meaning of the word? To paraphrase the verse, If I do everything that needs to be done, in order to secure an outcome, and the result comes out undesirable. On the other hand another person with the very same need does absolutely nothing to secure a desired result, but the end rewards him with a favourable outcome. How can anyone reconcile this?

The fact that, I having done everything expected of me, to guarantee successes means that, I could *not have done anything more* within my power to influence my desired result. The fact that the other party who did absolutely nothing to secure a desired outcome, except of course *being there in existence*, and still got rewarded, means that even his own slightest effort had he decided to do something, was of no effect upon the outcome. In both cases, it is evident that no effort of a person is of significance in the scenario.

So could this have happened on its own? Remember, nothing that ever happens on this planet or elsewhere for that matter is without cause. Even science argues strongly in support of this fact. Arriving at a conclusion that says something has no cause is just an escape from the truth. This would seek solace in the difficulty of proving the cause. However, we observe here, that something did happen, but without recognisable cause. Could it be, that there exists, other causes unbeknown to us? It looks like this becomes the only logical explanation if it's true that self-cause is a deception. There surely must be another source, causing these things to happen, a hidden hand perhaps.

This source as it seems, refuses to be governed and influenced by what we understand to be the requisite effort in this realm. It insists on its own 'illogical' ways. The results show that the source, which refuses to be governed by the laws of this existence, points to the fact that it may not be resident in this realm of humans, for if it was, it would be obliged to obey them. All this doing seems to point away from our reality to a 'power', beyond human power. Though it's a hidden hand, the evidence is overwhelming, that it can only be God. He seems to fit perfectly, into the attributes described here. So we can safely say man had absolutely nothing to do with the result that came to them. That's when we can say chance has happened. However, of the two, 'chance' happened to the recipient of the favourable news.

The most important condition for one to take full advantage of chance when it appears to them is to be there. I take it you are there somewhere. If you are reading this book, rejoice therefore, for you are alive and 'there' somewhere, for your chance will locate you and happen for you one of these days. The same way it is unpredictable in coming, by the same measure, it is uncertain, when it will happen to you. And should it happen to you; it is not guaranteed, not to, or to, happen ever again in your lifetime. Man shall always have to keep expecting for chance to come his way. For it can come and fail to be utilized properly. But it shall surely come, and in your lifetime. At the first sign of one's 'chance' unfolding, one must grab it and own it. Never make the mistake of missing your chance when it does come. For sometimes it might never come back again. Sometimes it makes the difference between a comfortable life and a miserable one. Our chances come differently. Some are blessed with more chances than are others. However, as *Ecclesiastes 10; 6-7* confirms, every man has his portion.

Chance happens within the confines of time. When it appears or happens in a man's life and is received, it accelerates your progress to a position where no one will have logical explanation to give with respect to where you find yourself. Though the cause of 'chance' is not physical, its manifestation is experienced in the physical world. The effects of 'chance' or the results cannot transcend the physical existence. It is only meant to enrich the physical life, but has no influence and is of no consequence in the after-world. That's the reason why it happens to all men regardless of what you believe. It does not require much from you except that you be alive, ready for it and grab it when it eventually comes.

Proverbs 22; 17 – 22 Bow down thine ear, and hear the words of the wise, and apply thine heart unto my knowledge.

18 For it is a pleasant thing if thou keep them within thee; they shall withal be fitted in thy lips.

19 that thy trust may be in the Lord, I have made known to thee this day, even to thee.

20 Have not I written to thee excellent things in counsels and knowledge?
21 That I might make thee know the certainty of the words of truth; that thou mightest answer the words of truth to them that send unto thee?

22 Rob not the poor, because he is poor: neither oppress the afflicted in the gate:

Life demands all human beings to work hard, toil and labour for survival. This requirement ensures the abundant supply of treasures gathered and stored up on earth to meet that demand. However, as fate would have it, when 'chance' happens to you, it has no regard of the requisite effort or lack of it on your part. Deserving or not, you will find yourself placed at a position that would ordinarily require years of toil and labour. In other words, chance buys you time. Chance is always preceded by investment in time, requisite effort, acquired skill and hard work done by somebody, who does not necessarily have to be identified, because remember, the earth and its fullness, all belong to God. He is the true owner of silver and gold.

So when chance happens to man, no matter at what point, you find yourself, it will bring you to a position of significance, as if rewarding you for the hard work deserving of such promotion. Another person, at the same level as you, in that new state, who did not get there by chance will have laboured and sweated and taken years to get there. That is 'chance', and it is one of God's legitimate apparatus that He uses to redeem lost time. So wherever you find yourself, which point may not be justifiable by way of reason and came by in the natural way of life is your chance and you should never let anyone despise that status, for it is authentic and God given.

Proverbs 16; 33 The lot is cast into the lap, but the whole disposing thereof is of the Lord.

God is in control. Whatever we define as chance, is just a deliberate act of God. May your chance come your way, and locate you, and when it does embrace it. It may linger for a period, but it will certainly not last forever.

Chapter 20
Time and Faith

Allow me a little while again to use a hypothetical situation to emphasise an important point. Let us suppose that we could convince God to reverse time all the way back to the moment when He created it. In the process, let us also pursue the character of faith as that happens. Assuming that the process starts, this very moment, and is travelling all the way back to the moment of its creation at the same rate it was passing. I would like to think that there is no definable pattern in the behaviour of 'faith' as 'time' approaches the beginning because as far as I understand, faith should work when time is moving in the correct direction, and though it has a starting point just as time has, faith only appears when activated. And like a spirit, it is confined to a vessel, which activates it. So at the point that time reaches its 'beginning' beyond that point, it cannot exist. Faith also should cease to exist. So the moment that time began, must have been the starting point of faith. What merit justifies its existence before 'time' and with nothing to actuate it? Before this event, only God existed, who had no need for it?

He is God and has no need for anything. He is self-sufficient. All things belong to him, and He does not need to hope for anything. He begets what He wants. I cannot imagine what beneficial purpose faith, would serve in an environment where only God existed. Besides, we have seen how efficient God's systems are; His creation was purposeful, and so would not create anything before its purpose was due. We can safely say that there was no space for faith before the beginning, the same way we eliminated the possibility of time existing in that same environment. What attracted faith or enticed it was the passage of the very first moment of time. The stroke of the subsequent moment of time, after the first, created an environment that allowed the possibility of faith to work.

In other words, a platform where faith could be invoked became, but still with nothing to activate it. Faith was crucial for man, in order to be able to live in the 'now'. The separations that we ascribe to time do not give room for 'the now' to exist, because once a moment comes, no matter how current, in real terms, that moment qualifies and rightly so, for a place in 'the past', and which-ever moment, that has not yet come, qualifies as the future. So where is room for now?

That is why we spoke about our existence on this earth as transitory. We can never live in the now, and yet we have to. That is the job of faith. So what faith does is that it brings those things that are in the future into my present time. So to sum this up, time had to come before faith, and faith was God's invention to deal with time. The frailty had to come before the remedy, again confirming the consistency of the logic, which God so religiously followed throughout His work. If that was the case, that God designed these things in that manner, then it would follow, that both time and faith were designed for man, for we know he had no need for them, and also that it is man, that inherited the new existence (after creation) and not God.

But just what for? God had a purpose for all His creations. Upon receiving this inheritance, it is interesting to note that, the very first words ever spoken by God to man, were a revelation about time, and in doing so planted the seed of faith in man. Let me explain. I believe that day was the day faith was made known and introduced to man. Because God knew that; *Faith cometh by hearing, and hearing by the word of God, Romans 10; 17*. So the first sermon ever preached on earth was a sermon to plant the seed of faith in man. This was a well calculated thought, because remember, the purpose of all creation was for His pleasure. And He knew that if this seed was not planted, He was never going to be pleased by man, for we know what *Hebrews 11; 6* says, *But without faith, it is impossible to please him.*

So apart from any other assignment given to it, faith is an apparatus that was crafted to cause God's pleasure. It means then that, if you walk in faith, your purpose is established, because otherwise, how else can one please God apart from fitting perfectly into His intended purpose for your life? For as long as God is pleased, you are doing the right thing and you are walking in faith.

Examining that scripture again of Genesis, in which God introduced faith to mankind by speaking. Like we said earlier, in this loaded verse God was speaking deep revelation to man. I have studied this verse for many times and from different scripture versions and came to the conclusion that there could not have been, a better way to begin this verse, than for God to use the command, "be." Notice how God begins the instruction to the person he had just created, who at that moment was still in a state of 'perfection', with the semblance of God in all respects, you would think that this was the ideal man.

But nonetheless, God makes a striking revelation when He gave the command, which I shall seek your permission to paraphrase. 'Though I have been pleased to let you pass into existence, as you are, there however, exists an advanced form of you in another reality', which I am commanding you now to become.' But this advanced existence could not have been in the 'now' moment because man had to become it first. Which meant that, at that moment that reality had not yet come. But if God confirmed it then it must have been there somewhere. And God knew what he was talking about, because *Isaiah 46; 10 declaring the end from the beginning, and from ancient times the things that are not yet done, saying My counsel shall stand, and I will do all my pleasure:*

So He makes the command, "Be fruitful...." Remember, that this command was being directed towards a brand-new man, prompting the question; why He would, knowingly create a being, and upon completing the job, give him a command to become something else supposedly better? Moreover, He had a detailed vision of what the man must become.

My question then is why didn't he just create a 'complete' man, with all the qualities He desired, than create him, then start commanding him to become something else immediately after creating him? Our knowledge of the omniscience of God persuades us to believe there must have been a good reason as to why He did that. Clearly with all the necessary information and capacity at his disposal, He still made a choice to settle for what we question right now. If you study carefully, the story of creation, you will discover that upon every completed work by God, in-fact six times during creation, we read the statement that; *'and God saw that it was good'*. However, that statement never surfaced when man was created, as if to answer His critics. He definitely knew what He was doing. It looks like God was still not done with man. In a subtle way, He was pointing man towards a purposeful position. And that is why 'purpose', has never been so apparent. You have to discover and develop it yourself and in the process become all that God has commanded you to become.

God could not have fulfilled man's purpose by creating an already fruitful and multiplied man. This was man's portion to perform. Now purpose was locked, and would unfold in time. For purpose to make sense the duration of its usefulness must be predetermined, otherwise anything that goes on forever is without purpose. So the moment that an expected end had been revealed to man, hope, was immediately ignited in him. At that moment, when hope appeared, man became fully equipped to respond to the command of becoming a purposeful being.

All the necessary conditions required to fulfill the command had now been created. Time came first, and when man had come, a complete platform for faith to work also came to life, God then, planted the first seed of faith in man by speaking a word, and when man had heard, faith was born and with it, came hope to accomplish the purpose of becoming fruitful and purposeful.

The last verse of **Genesis 1** finally admits after all this had been acomplished, saying: *"And God saw everything that he had made, and behold; it was very good"*

So Work Your Faith

As we have just seen, God himself entrusted us with the task of self-empowerment, which task He is confident we are more than capable of handling. He has equipped us with all the faculties required to take it up. This one is in our hands dear   friends, and we have very little choice. Remember, it was given as a command. We agreed that purpose is the ultimate reason for any existence; therefore, obedience to the giver of purpose determines how well we do in life.

Psalm 37:23. The steps of a good man are ordered by the Lord: and he delighteth in his way.

Work your faith! that way you safeguard your every step of your life. Like 'chance', the effect that faith has in a man's life is to leave a man in a position of advancement. The requirement though for faith to work in a man's life is quite different from that of chance. In fact, it is the total opposite. For faith to work for you, it has everything to do with yourself. You have to work your faith and develop it. If you do not, then time shall always solidly stand in your way, because time is the barrier that separates your two worlds; your present realities and your desired future. The stronger your faith grows; the least significant time becomes for you.

Unwavering faith takes dominion over 'time' always. The more you begin to visualise your desired future and as you embrace it; your faith begins to draw it to you. You behold what you don't yet have and have the feeling of experiencing it, as though you already have it, If this is done enough times and consistently, 'time' itself has no choice but to give in to your faith.

Faith is a powerful tool for man to fight time and conquer it. So it means, you have to master your mind and condition your thoughts to bring the reality you want from that distant future to your present life. Unlike chance, faith puts you in a position of advancement, by hauling the desired picture from the future to your present time. Your thoughts are the medium which frames that reality, but are often bombarded with many negative feelings, which create 'doubt' and fight your faith. Doubt, is an enemy of faith. When you allow it to grow, it weakens our faith, and 'solidifies' time. This makes it that much more difficult to bring your future realities closer to you. Work out your faith and time will always bow down to you.

Chapter 21
Exist past your physical time.

Finding yourself 'space' to exist past your lifetime

Maybe you are wondering how legacy and mentorship fits into all this. Yes! legacy that's what I am talking about! I know what you are now saying. 'It means one must die first?' Yes, that's the only way you can leave an enduring one. And that is the context we want to deal with in this chapter. If you do leave one, and yet you are still alive, it means you are no longer found where you left it. It has something to do, with you no longer being present. I found some synonyms of that word quite interesting, and I thought they would help qualify the foregoing statement. Here is the list: hangover, remnant, residue, leftover, etc. of you. It is a fact, known to every man that, the duration of our lives on earth will soon come to an end. It means that our time on earth is limited. Sooner or later, whether we like it or not, the reality of our lives fading away is sure to manifest. So faced by this threat, of dying, and dying quickly, man became desperate not only to live, but as legacy would testify; to even live forever if possible.

And so man in realising this, has relentlessly attempted to circumvent their earthly limit. If they could, they would certainly have found a remedy for this 'shortness' of their time on earth. Knowledge that death is fact also pushed man to devise ways that would guarantee continued existence in whatever form possible, even after it came. That's legacy. The length of time that your legacy will allow you to live depends on how much of it (this short time) you have invested into building that legacy. This means, that your level of desperation to live longer should motivate your effort to build one now, which in-turn determines how far into the future it will thrive. Legacy is about influence. The opening statement in the book 'Nurturing Champions' by Dr Makoni says, *"Without a doubt,*
the uppermost questing of the human spirit is to increase its influence and impact past one's lifetime."

Some people have worked so hard on increasing their influence, to the extent that though they might have passed on, for decades, or even centuries, their influence is much stronger than the presence of us that could be still. Let me raise an argument, which might appear to be controversial or hard to swallow: that influence is better than physical presence if purpose is lost. Remember, we said that, your time on earth, whatever you are, is linked to your purpose. If time is really as short, then if we are to increase our influence enough, it means, there is not enough time during our lives to live outside our purpose and then make a meaningful impact, because the influence we will exert at the end can only propel our legacy a limited distance. It is the men who lived in their purpose that created lasting legacies.

If you still don't know yours, those that have gone before you would look better. They would have lived in theirs (purpose), and would overtake you by their influence. Can you see that through influence, they still live and perform works and still make achievements just as the living? Their families are still fed from the power of their influence, yet we who are alive suffer. The irony of it all is that it's happening in borrowed time. Can we not say that these people still live? In 1999, Time magazine selected Albert Einstein as Person of the Century, but although one could say it could be subjective, just the fact that in your time he is still that competent enough to even be recognised ahead of the living means that his influence continues to thrive. We can go on and on giving examples of these long-gone champions who to this day still exert great influence. I would like to go further and say that, even when alive, your influence is generally more powerful than your physical presence, because your physical presence in the end reveals your weaknesses, which your influence would not display.

Let's take the example of a strict school head, just the mention of his name is enough to enforce discipline among his students, but it would surprise you to observe that his own presence would not foster as much discipline because he may decide to take a softer stance for whatever reason, which influence would not have tolerated. Is it not better, to exist by influence rather than presence? So if influence is that important, why do we live as if it is of no significance? Why don't you start building your own legacy? It is a deliberate action that takes time to build, but that time will be released when you are gone. Make up your mind today and propel your time well into the future, to allow you to live long after you are physically gone. Besides it is the only way you can recover lost time using your own effort. I will end this chapter by saying, a life well lived, leaves a trace. How you use your time now, will witness for you before God and man will remember your works.

Chapter 22
The reward of long life

"There is but a span between the cradle and the grave. Solomon said, "there is a time to be born and a time to die Ecclesiastes 3; 2 - but mentions no time of living – as if that it were so short, it were not worth speaking of." Sermon by Thomas Watson

In-fact, the bible is awash with scriptures that confirm just how short our time on earth is. It is therefore, amazing, that we often have to be reminded of this truth, as sometimes we tend to live so recklessly like as if one would live forever. Is the memory of man so short that God has to constantly remind him? Or is it so important that God couldn't afford not to remind us? If God, who himself is not affected by this brevity of time, places such weight upon it, how much more for us, whose time could be terminated any moment, even this very moment? To make emphasis and drive home the point, we shall pick just a few scriptures written by different authors and coming from both the old and the new testaments.

Psalms 39; 5 Behold, thou hast made my days as a handbreadth; and mine age is as nothing before thee. Verily, every man at his best state is altogether vanity. Se'lah.

Job 14; 1 Man that is born of a woman is of a few days, and full of trouble.

1 Corinthians 7; 29 But this I say, brethren, the time is short

Psalms 89; 47 remember how short my time is

Job 7; 9 as the cloud is consumed and vanisheth away: so he that goeth down to the grave shall come up no more.

I hope these few verses, have managed to dislodge doubt in your minds, if you still had any, and confirmed too, that a man's life is indeed short. That scenario almost seems to seal humanity's fate as being perpetually subordinate to time, but as we said earlier, God has created means to help man to control the way 'time' affects their lives. Each one of us has been apportioned an appointed time to live and the boundaries are determined by Him. However, God has granted us a special privilege of being able to determine whether we can live beyond that point or not. Anyone who foregoes this privilege is sure not to live any moment longer than was set for him, for certain deliberate actions have to be taken by man, to activate the extension of their time on earth. The choice is ours, and an extension of our time is ours to grab from the jaws of time.

How can I determine that my time on earth is extended?

God has laid conditions for man to fulfill in order for them to take advantage of the leeway that He has given them, to be able to elude the boundaries of time set for them and receive an extension to their lives. If you remember earlier we agreed that God has placed such value on His word to the extent that He has elevated it above everything else. Put in another way, God has put His 'head on the block' for His word. That is His confidence in it. *Jeremiah 1; 12* suggested that He will watch over it in order to actualise it. More-so, in cases that stand to threaten or disrupt the fulfillment of promises made in His word for our lives, He stands resolute in defense so as to protect His own character and reputation, because He cannot be labeled a liar. His promises are unfailing as a result. Whatever God has promised; it shall come to pass.

Now God has promised long life, or more days, or more time, to those that fulfill the requirements set out in his word. There are several conditions laid out in order for that reward to come true. If you aspire to be a candidate to receive this reward, you have to be prepared to take on the challenge.

So, that means, the reward for long life is not for everyone, but to as many as are willing to receive it and are prepared to do what it takes to have it. Every promise of God has a premise; there are conditions to be fulfilled first.

How then do I get the reward of long life?

Obey God and the reward is yours to take, remember we interrogated obedience much earlier? And there we agreed that the space between where you find yourself today, and where you ought to be right now, is covered by obedience. The good thing about this reward is that, it too falls in the category of the many promises made by God. As long as you have done your side of the bargain, you can hold God to account based on His word which He has promised to perform. If you are so desirous to exist, past your set time boundaries in your physical state, here are the things you have to do to be blessed in that manner.

Fear the Lord

Proverbs 9; 10-12 - The fear of the Lord is the beginning of wisdom, for by me thy days shall be multiplied, and the years of thy life shall be increased. If thou be wise, thou shalt be wise for thyself

Proverbs 10; 27 - The fear of the Lord prolongeth days: but the years of the wicked shall be shortened.

Psalms128; 1-6 blessed is every one that feareth the Lord; that walketh in his ways Yea, thou shalt see thy children's children, and peace upon Israel.

The scriptures here reveal that wisdom is the condition that brings the reward. But how do you get wisdom? – The fear of the Lord. And yet we know that, the fear of the Lord is what causes wisdom. Which brings me to say, wisdom adds length to life, and foolishness causes life to be cut short. If you want the benefit of a long life, seek wisdom.

Honour your parents

Exodus 20; 12 Honour thy father and thy mother: that thy days maybe long upon the land which the Lord thy God giveth thee.

Proverbs 3; 1-2 "My son, forget not my law; but let thine heart keep my commandments: For length of days, and long life, and peace, shall they add to thee".

Proverbs 4; 10 – Hear, O my son, and receive my sayings; and the years of thy life shall be many.

From these scriptures, it appears, there is a strong correlation between long life and honouring our parents. It looks like God has locked the blessing of long life in the quality of relationship we share with our parents. In-fact He has given it as a command, and as such implies that there is no exception, because if it's a commandment, then it applies to all of us. It is sin; therefore, not to honour our parents, and consequently; it becomes sinful to fail to live a longer life on account of disrespecting or shaming our parents. That means, this was given as an open ticket for all to be rewarded by long life. And because it is a reward, it comes with the benefit of prosperity. God would not add more years of misery, but years full of happiness. How simple can it get? You desire a long life? Just honour your parents.

Obey God's commands and walk in his ways

1 Kings 3; 14 – And if thou wilt walk in my ways, to keep my statutes and my commandments, as thy father David did walk, then I will lengthen thy days.

Proverbs 16; 31 The hoary head is a crown of glory; if it be founding the way of righteousness.

Psalms 91; 16 With long life will I satisfy him and show him my salvation.

Remember that we said the whole purpose of creation, was for the pleasure of the creator. If the creator is pleased, the task of delivering long life to you is not burdensome to Him. It comes naturally to him; He does not need to think about it; it is already programmed in his system. And since this is a promise from the almighty God, it is sure to happen. Test him and walk in his ways.

But just how long can this added time be?

Now brethren, when God gives, He gives freely and in abundance. His reward is well worth receiving in-case you are not convinced of its advantage. Firstly, if you examine carefully the duration of the added period, most of the scriptures we have referred to talk of years of added time, in- fact they refer to many years. If you recall, we said our time on earth is the most important time of our existence, because our position in eternity depends upon it. A day longer on earth is a great opportunity to buttress our chances of living a glorious life with the eternal King. So cherish every moment you wake up to a new day. It is a reminder that God has favoured you and loves you enough to give you yet another chance to prepare well, both for your family and for life ahead.

In *2 Kings 20*; *1*, we read that the prophet Isaiah, was sent to King Hezekiah to warn him, to put his house in order, because, he was going to die. He was greatly favoured to receive, such warning; because the majority of 'us' will never receive even the slightest clue of our imminent departure. That also means, it is very likely that the majority of 'us' will depart earth when we are ill prepared for it. So for those not favoured with such privilege, let each day that comes your way be your warning. Remember also that the status we shall assume in that afterlife depends on how much we prepared for it, on the earth.

Secondly our physical life is also enriched. His reward of long life is much more than a day, and if you read well, the long life is always accompanied with prosperity. Which means, apart from preparing for eternity, God also expects you to flourish on earth while you live! One scripture even says, with long life, I will satisfy you. That means, there must be a deep questing in man to exist forever if it was possible, and it is that questing, that God answers by satisfying us with long life. In the passage we have just referred to, Hezekiah exhibited that questing. It says he turned his face to the wall and cried to the Lord as it dawned on him that his life was coming to an end. As he cried, we notice that he held God to His word and reminded Him that he had fulfilled all of those conditions we listed above, and as such qualified for the reward of long life.

We can conclude too that he was obedient to his parents on the grounds that there is no evidence, to the contrary, and more so, that he became heir to his father's throne. He was rewarded with 15 more years. It is believed that he died of natural causes at the age of 54, which marked the end of his reign. However, imagine what 'mileage' the reward of long life gave him. It did not only come with 15 more years of life, but also accompanied by a successful reign, that is regarded as incomparable to any of his time. Decide for yourself based on this account whether it is worth it to work to receive this reward. Is it something you can aspire to do in your life time? I would certainly say, it is well worth toiling for. Imagine how much you can achieve in such a time. The ball is in your court. Long life is there for you to take. And closely linked to that is resurrection. Let's now turn to it for a few moments.

Resurrection, convince God

Linked to that, it is not unheard of, for God to change his mind even past the boundaries of your time to restore it back to you. He sets the boundaries, and it is well within his power if moved to, to shift them as he pleases. The challenge here is the kind of action that we can do that would catch the attention of the creator, and cause Him to change his mind, about shifting the boundaries of your life. The unfortunate part in the case of resurrection is that the one whose life is gone, or whose time has expired, has no say in the matter. Another, who is still in his time, has to stand in the gap and argue his case with God. He has to present an argument and justify why the departed life deserves continued existence. In other words, why they would deserve an extra 'slot' of time on earth?

The key here, is that the intercessor has to have enough grounds or basis on which to argue for your continued existence, with the Creator. I shall not dwell much on this point, because, there is little that one has to do, in order to be resurrected, but it is well worth knowing that we can still 'cheat' time by this method. What I can say in concluding this matter is that, have a good standing with God always and with fellow believers to pave the way for good grounds for your brethren to pray for your resurrection and that way, time can be shamed in your own life.

Chapter 23
Time to Conclude

In coming to my conclusion to this book, I would like to recall to your memory, the very thoughts that provoked the creation of this work. I feel it is of utmost importance to do so, because without them, we would not have seen the birth of this book. We have gone far afield, in trying to satisfy these very thoughts. For a long time I battled to understand why I seemed to always suffer defeat, whenever I had a face-to-face encounter with 'time'. I am now more enlightened and equipped to know how to deal with it, without causing frustration to myself, simply because I now understand the extent to which I can successfully challenge it. I am now conscious as well of the boundaries that I cannot cross in my struggle with it. I now know that certain objectives we have set for ourselves against time in the past are not attainable because we lacked knowledge of this thing called 'time'.

Not only that, it also baffled my mind, why even the seemingly successful people in life reveal during their last moments, how so unfulfilled and unconvinced they were, about the way they have lived and used their time. Even the great King Solomon ended up with a lament over the meaninglessness of everything under the sun. If you study his testimony, it bears witness to two things. Firstly, that the nature of our existence on earth is impermanent and short-lived, and secondly that the time spent on earth even having everything that you ever desire to have still does not satisfy a certain part of man's life. That part is not addressed by the level of physical success you achieved while you lived. Why after such a life would one start questioning life? As if there was more than they could have done to eliminate this regret. This to me supports the position taken in this book that 'time' as it pertains to a man's life, has two components to its purpose, which we have defined as the physical, which relates to our life on earth, and the spiritual, which takes care of our afterlife.

A human being has to strike a balance between these two during his lifetime. Satisfying one side only, is no good to them, because it is incomplete according to the purpose for which God established time, and results in the loss of both in the end.

No one can ever run away from this because, it was designed that way for all men, whether you believe it or not. We have seen how, before anything was ever created, God had already a plan for all his creations and how his thoughts would be revealed in his creation, in a way that they would comprehend, and 'time' was chosen to carry that mandate. The spiritual component of 'time' derives its strength from God's plan to redeem humanity, for the salvation of their souls, which he planned well before the foundations of the world. Which means, according to God, man, should never allow his time to lapse, before, the salvation of his soul as He intended. Make that resolution today, before your time is over. It cannot be overlooked by any human being, without creating serious consequence for himself. Time is an opportunity given to man, to 'improve the quality of his own' life in both 'worlds.' It is a precious commodity to all, because no one moment can pass a man twice. It is scarce, and gets even scarcer with each passing moment. It was designed, never to retreat, slow down, stop or be manipulated in any way, by any person. It is the most resolute creation of God in its assignment.

Though man lost dominion over it, God still intended that man triumphed over time, and so did not allow a situation where man would be entirely and perpetually subjugated and became hopeless against it. He designed ways in which it could be kept at bay, but certainly ensured that any such action would now require his involvement. Man now had to rely on God, to regain, his lost authority. It's a fact that should be made clear that without God, it is not possible to defeat and that is the quandary that the 'independent' man finds himself in.

Time is an opportunity for your future. Improve every minute of it. Never let a day pass without depositing into that future. And if it's always about the future, it therefore, calls for faith, because faith speaks to the future. Any moment allowed to pass without adding value to it, leads to an accumulation of armory against our own lives, which we purport to love. If you ever find yourself at any moment in your life, doing something that does not support your future time, let it occur to you that, that is what constitutes wastage of your time. Always remember, that time may never be redeemed again.   You need to stop right away, and channel your energy into those things that reward your future. Don't let the young 'you' leave all the work for the old you. Each life allowed to exist deserves a blissful experience on earth and a blissful life, after life on earth. The choice is in your hands. Choose this day, to live a purposeful life, and align your energies to that purpose.   Managing time becomes easier as waste of time can almost be eliminated because all efforts pointing to your purpose add value.

Discover that purpose, do what it takes to live in it. If that becomes your goal, time can never be lost. To the young, I say, time is an asset that any elderly can never possess. You are loaded more than any elderly person around you, regardless of their standing. Choose to value and respect the advantage you have over them today. Revise your attitude and see what positive direction your life will take. Whatever your father can't do because of age, do it with stubborn determination. Seize the moment, and ride on the tide, knowing that one day it shall subside. No excuse is good enough to justify wasted time, and wasted opportunity, no matter how legitimate your excuse may sound to you. You are responsible for your own time. Do not be caught up in the trap or philosophy of 'busy for nothing'. It always leads to a state of finding good excuses for lost time on the deception that "I was busy."

Weigh the results by costing the lost opportunities, then you can objectively judge if the 'busy' was worth the while. The judgement over your time will always fall on you unfortunately. So be resolute about your own time management, and face the judgement for what you, rather than someone else have done. The power that you feel today is depleted tomorrow. If you omitted to do a necessary thing today that means tomorrow the load is heavier, because tomorrow has its own load. Do what you have to do today; today. In fact, lets come up with a slogan that shall always be a reminder for us never to procrastinate. Whenever you feel the edge to always remind yourself of this slogan. "DO NOW"

To the mature and grown up, you have graduated from the period of hard work. Thank God if during that time you did your part. It means you burden is lighter today. If not, your conditions are much more difficult, but remember, God has designed ways to redeem our time. Work on your faith, build your legacy. Deposit in someone, a part of you that you want to see live forever. Pray for long life to allow you to see through all these tasks. As you retreat to a slower paced life, realise too that you now approach the end of your time. When life on earth approaches the end, a new life is dawning. What better thing to do now than devote the remaining time to preparing oneself for the next life. Time was given for that purpose also, and it will be sad to live to that age and fail to take advantage of the opportunity.

To all those whom we specifically pointed out, make amends. Correct your shortcomings and start living a purposeful life. If you find you still have time to spare in life, I can guarantee you that this is a sign that your purpose is still not clear. There is never time to spare. Every minute is taken and that is when we have to start learning and employing time management skills as taught and suggested in this book.

The approach we have taken in this book is to come up with a strategy that spans your entire life, or the entire life of your business. Break down the bigger picture into smaller and manageable tasks that gradually move you towards realising your goals. Have a clear roadmap of where you are going. Set milestones, which will guide your progress. That is exactly how God Himself did it. He had a plan for all His creation, which covered the whole life of the universe.

He set milestones to allow for tracking His progress. So the biggest 'take away' of this book is to learn and copy from the strategy of God himself. He is the chief strategist of all things.

May God help you as you embark on a new journey to manage your time with the few insights you picked from this book. Be thoroughly Blessed.

The end

To everything,

there is a season,

and a TIME

to every purpose under the heaven:

www.ingramcontent.com/pod-product-compliance
Lightning Source LLC
Chambersburg PA
CBHW051909170526
45168CB00001B/304